RIGHT WAY
TO
APPLY
FOR A
JOB

RIGHT WAY TO
APPLY
FOR A
JOB

(originally published as 'How to Face That Interview')

by
Arthur Wilcox,
B.Sc., B.Sc. (Econ.), M.Ed.

PAPERFRONTS

ELLIOT RIGHT WAY BOOKS
KINGSWOOD, SURREY, U.K.

Printed and bound in Great Britain by Cox & Wyman Ltd,
Reading

For
SYLVIA
who helped in lots of ways

CONTENTS

PART I

We begin with school-leavers. But if you've left school far behind, don't let that deter you. You may pick up some useful tips.

PART II

Here we deal with more sophisticated job-hunting.

Introduction

This book will help all who seek a job, whether a first job, a better job or merely a different one. It is of special use to those who are unemployed, and will also benefit those seeking a place on a Government-sponsored training (or re-training) scheme. The ideas which the book gives will assist the interview technique of those seeking entry to university.

Job-hunting has a high built-in failure rate. When six candidates are interviewed for one job, five must be rejects. Yet these five are among the best in the field.

How can an applicant prevent the long odds against him from sapping his confidence? Answers to this question are particularly important for the school leaver who has worked his way up the school and achieved a position of some responsibility and perhaps some authority, and whose first experience of trying to enter the confusing and competitive world of work marks him down as a 'failure'. They are no less vital for the person who has lost his job and may face a long period on the unemployment register unless he goes into action quickly and effectively.

He might shorten the odds by putting in for as many jobs as he can. If he adopts this hit-or-miss practice, he will get a job in the end, but his disappointment may start when he realizes that it is the wrong job.

The best thing he can do is to study the market for jobs in his particular line and in his own locality (or further afield, if he is prepared to move), to select his targets realistically, and to prepare his written application and his performance at interview with the utmost care.

The more efficiently he presents himself – on paper and in personal contact – the better will be his showing in the labour market. He can rest assured that an employer is just as anxious to pick the right worker as he is to pick the right job.

Interviewers of all levels and ages of applicant sometimes

find that they have regretfully to turn down candidates with a great deal to commend them. Their reasons for rejecting a candidate might begin:

'I liked him, but ...'

'Why didn't anyone advise him ...'

'Didn't he realize that ...'

'What a pity he hasn't got (some qualification or ancillary subject, certain experience, or some personal quality vital for the job)'.

They might end by saying 'He'll make a good career somewhere, but not with us'.

Often, these things can't be helped. At interview it's too late. You can't produce a missing qualification especially for interview, nor gain precious experience, but you can at least prepare yourself and show yourself to best advantage.

The worst case of all, because it could so easily have been remedied, is that of the person who possesses all the basic qualifications, experience and know-how, and enough of the personal qualities to make him a fair prospect, but who somehow doesn't present himself well at interview.

This might not matter in a poor field, but it does matter when it is a toss-up between two or more candidates. It could so easily turn out that the worse is picked and the better rejected, simply because the former comes over more positively. The fact that he comes over positively is, of course, in his favour, but performance at interview does not represent faithfully the qualities needed in the job itself.

To be sure, the rejected candidate, like the selected one, knew in advance that the interview was a crucial situation. Crucial or not, for many people it is rather an unknown situation, hedged with speculation, rumour, gossip, fears, and something of a mythology. What the interviewer thinks, what he is like, what he really wants, what the interplay between interviewer and interviewee is going to be like and the course it will take – all these are unknown. All the same, a candidate can prepare himself, and think out likely eventualities in advance. Careful preparation may spare a candidate regrets later on.

This book is designed to help candidates prepare themselves for interview. Interviews can take several forms. This book assumes a single interviewer facing a single candidate. The substance and course of an interview are not greatly changed if there are two interviewers or a panel of them. (Group interviews bring in further factors with which this book does not attempt to deal.)

Unemployment

Since this book was first published, unemployment has increased enormously throughout the Western World. Any recovery in economic activity may well *not* produce a corresponding increase in employment opportunities because of the impact of high technology. Fewer workers will be needed, but they will be more efficient and more flexible.

This is bringing a change in career patterns. There is more retraining. 'A job for life' is becoming a thing of the past. Career structures within companies are altering and internal development schemes are increasingly taking the place of 'paper' qualifications (provided the minimum standards are achieved.)

It is likely that opportunities in the future will go to those who can learn new skills and adapt to the changed requirements of the labour market.

Examinations of an applicant's 'track record' combined with an interview assessment remains the traditional way of choosing. Thus the applicant must prepare a plan to display his or her experience – and potential – to best advantage.

The book, therefore, contains useful advice for candidates for interview at whatever level; from the raw school-leaver looking for his first job or sparring for selection to a job experience scheme to the professional person looking for a better one. Wherever you come in this spectrum, it should give you some of the know-how and confidence you need.

It starts, where we all start, with the school leaver.

PART I

Finding that Job

STAGE ONE: SEEKING INFORMATION

While you are still at school

School library
  (i) Careers books and pamphlets.
 (ii) Booklets setting out career prospects with local firms and industries.
(iii) Books of a general nature which throw some light on careers.

School staff
 (i) Teachers of particular subjects will know about employment prospects of young people who have followed courses in those subjects and have perhaps gained qualifications in them.
(ii) There may be a careers teacher on the staff of your school. He may be full-time or, more likely, part-time. If there is no careers teacher, the Head, Deputy Head, or perhaps a Housemaster may give careers advice. If there is no teacher who you feel can help you, and no notice referring to careers on the notice board, try the school office. Quite often a school establishes a useful connection with local firms. A firm may inquire whether the school can recommend a promising boy or girl in their particular line of business. Or it can work the other way round: a Head who knows that boys or girls in the past have done well with particular firms, may recommend likely leavers to these firms. Either way round, the school office is a 'clearing house' for information and perhaps actual applications.

Services offered by or through the school

(i) Visiting speakers who talk about employment prospects in commerce, industry, and the various services. Their help is not limited to a lecture. They answer questions, leave pamphlets or other hand-outs for reading at leisure, and organize personal contact where this is called for.

(ii) Visits by groups of young people to various places of work. These are specially important because they can see for themselves and ask questions on the spot. Such visits are often brief, but they are sometimes extended to provide valuable work experience in an authentic setting.

(iii) Leavers' conferences (under this or some other name) by which leavers (and their parents, if the meetings are held in the evening) hear about job or Further Education prospects in the locality. These are useful occasions for meeting representatives of firms and other bodies to discuss practical matters.

(iv) Meetings with Careers Officers and school staff connected with employment.

Looking after your personal interests

(i) Find out what jobs are possible with your interests, the courses you have followed at school, and exam and other achievements.

(ii) Find out what jobs you are interested in, but are ruled out for you because you haven't the right qualifications. Can you make up any missing qualifications if you are really keen on one of these jobs?

(iii) Discuss with anyone able and willing to help you the pros and cons of the various jobs you are interested in. Don't let anyone make up your mind for you. All the same, take advice seriously, from whatever quarter it comes. From all the possibilities, you must narrow the choice to one! (You will find in practice that there are all sorts of limitations on your choices: e.g. the employement situation in your locality.)

Don't forget to contact a few of those who are a year or two older than you are, and are already at work, so you can be guided by the practical experience of people who were once in your position. They will be able to tell you of unexpected snags that turned up, as well as things that went unexpectedly well.

While you are still at school/when you have left school

Local library

(i) Careers books.

(ii) Use the library's information service. The library offers a wider service than you might suspect. Where they cannot provide the sort of detailed information you might want, they are able to put you in touch with organizations, firms, etc., who can.

(iii) The library will almost certainly have a wider range of local newspapers than you take at home. Look through the advertisements offering jobs.

(iv) Study local directories and the 'yellow pages' of the telephone directory to see what firms there are of the sort you want.

(v) See if there are local Schools/Industry liaison groups providing contact between Head Teachers and senior industrialists. Some of these provide additional resource centres in libraries and schools.

STAGE TWO: ACTING ON YOUR INFORMATION

(i) Learning about likely jobs from advertisements, the Careers Service, personal contact, etc., and telephoning for an interview or sending in an application.

(ii) Telephoning, writing, or calling at the premises of a likely firm (or office, etc.) even though no job is at present being advertised. You will get an idea of when one may turn up for a person of your age and qualifications. You may get a useful insight into the way young people are taken on, by talking to the personnel officer (or training officer, or education officer, etc.) of a large concern.

(iii) When a job is really on the cards, mount your own personal 'campaign' for achieving it, using the advice given in this book. Your campaign will be, at its simplest, a telephone call arranging for an appointment, your own self-preparation, and the interview. At a higher level, it will include sending for an application form (or writing your own application if there is no form), getting your testimonials and exam certificates ready, arranging for referees, preparing yourself for interview and making a success of it when it comes.

(iv) Don't be afraid to have out two or more applications at the same time. You must look after your own interests here, and you can't afford to let time slip by while a firm is considering an application from you.

(v) In consultation with the Careers Office, you may be able (through the Youth Training Scheme) to obtain work experience with a particular employer whose work suits you, and this could lead to permanent employment later.

How Far can Parents Help?

Many schools hold careers conventions (or conferences) at which parents and young people together can learn, from the people concerned, about prospects in local industry and commerce, and in various other occupations. Such meetings are exploratory, and questions can be asked and interest shown without the young people committing themselves in any way.

Parents are a real help here, because they can often ask more knowledgeable questions than their children can, and follow them up on their children's behalf. At a careers convention it is the representatives of firms, etc., who are on show rather than the young people themselves. They are as anxious to put their kind of work in a good light as candidates are to show themselves attractively. If it comes to it, the school leaver (or his parents) can put them through the same kind of grilling as he himself may fear, drawing out the details of just what they want to know.

It might seem as though the role of parents could be the same in an interview situation as it is at a careers convention. After all, the parents could chip in at an interview, adding support to their son's (or daughter's) case, prompting him with points he might be too forgetful or too timid to put on his own behalf, and asking the interviewer exactly those questions to which the young person ought to have the answers but is unlikely to ask himself. Young people's horizons rarely stretch beyond the next twelve months, and they can easily overlook some less immediate things that may turn out to be quite vital to them.

In fact, though, it can be rather risky having parents at interview. The boy (or girl) would be 'on show' twice over: before the interviewer, and before one or both of his parents. The triangular relationship might easily be a deterrent to frankness. Two results can easily occur: the wrong decision might be made, and recriminations could easily follow when the interview is over and the boy is with his parents again. It cuts the other way, though. A boy can feel friendless and alone facing an authoritative and experienced interviewer with his own immaturity and sketchy knowledge. The contrast is all the sharper if anything happens to suggest (wrongly) that the boy and his interviewer are somehow antagonists.

A first interview (like first love) can seem a traumatic experience at the time. (If it does not appear like this, it might be because the candidate takes it too lightly, or doesn't realize its importance; in most cases, though, the shock is softened by preparation on the part of the candidate.) In an advisory interview, or any meeting that does not commit you, parental support may well be a help, but for the interview where you commit yourself the most sensible advice is: Go it alone.

Writing about that Job

First impressions count, and the first impression that your future employer gains of you comes from your letter applying for the job or asking for an appointment. How do you want to appear to him? It is worth taking trouble to present this preview of yourself as attractively as possible.

On page 66, I shall explain how to apply for a job where we are dealing with candidates seeking professional posts or trying to improve their job by moving to another one.

Much of what I say, therefore, applies to your application for a first job, and there is no harm in presenting a c.v. (Curriculum Vitae) which means details about yourself, your qualifications and achievements, your past employment (if any) and your interests, etc.

Who are you?

Obviously the person who has been at work for some time has got more of a track record and his c.v. could be quite a comprehensive and detailed document, although it should never exceed one side of a type-written page.

For the school-leaver the track record is more difficult since you have not got much experience yet, but everybody has some sort of experience that is useful information for a prospective employer.

Make up a c.v. including in it all the matters of general interest which could be useful information to any prospective employer. Then, when you apply for a job, all you need to do is to write a short letter to accompany the c.v.

Draw up your c.v. with care, if possible getting a friend or relative to type it out, and get some copies made at the local copy shop.

The c.v. should contain the following:–

1. **Name, Address and Telephone Number (if any).**
2. **Date of Birth.**
3. **Schools attended.**

4. **Examination results, especially 'O' Levels or C.S.E.s.**
5. **Details of any part-time or Saturday jobs which you have done.**
6. **Details of any hobbies or interests especially if these might be useful adjuncts to employment.**
7. **Details of any sports interests or other pastimes such as music.**
8. **Details of any organisations you belong to.**
9. **It may also be useful to say if you have got a motorbike or bicycle since employers often prefer an applicant from nearby than one from farther away who would have to rely on public transport.**

Such a c.v. might end up looking like this:-

Name: Cynthia Joan Smith (Miss)
Address: 14 High Road, Plumtree, Nottinghamshire.
　　　　 NG14 6WW.
Telephone: Plumtree (06077) 55522
Date of Birth: 19.4.XX
Schools:　a) educated in Scotland at Livingstone Primary School.
　　　　　 b) Plumtree Comprehensive School
　　　　　　　(Headmaster: Mr R. V. Rathbone, B.Sc., to whom reference may be made).

Examination Results:
'O' Level Mathematics Grade B
'O' Level Physics Grade C
C.S.E. Geography Grade 1
C.S.E. English Grade 3
C.S.E. Economics Grade 3
C.S.E. Home Economics Grade 1

For the last three years I have done a paper round for Mr. Johnson of Johnsons Newsagency, 6 High Street, Plumtree.

During the last year I have worked on Saturdays at Sainsbury's 29 Wheeler Gate, Nottingham at restocking the shelves and assisting in the Butchery Department.

I played for the 2nd Eleven Hockey Team of Plumtree

Comprehensive School during last season and I am the School javelin champion.

I am a member of Plumtree Youth Club and I have also helped with Sunday School teaching at Plumtree United Reformed Church. I am also the reserve organist.

I am the owner of a reliable bicycle (and enjoy riding) and I am hoping to get a moped as soon as I can afford it.
(Date)

Send a letter with it

All that is needed to accompany this c.v. is a short letter applying for the job. In this letter, say:
  a) Which job you are applying for (there may be several advertised by big firms).
  b) When you are available for interview and perhaps
  c) Names, addresses and telephone numbers of referees who might speak up on your behalf.

The lay-out on the page should be correct with a proper margin on the left-hand side. Remember what you were taught at school about paragraphing. Do not cram your letter into a small space on the page, and try to keep the lines of your writing a uniform distance apart.

Make sure that your handwriting is easy to read, and if your spelling is poor, get someone else to check you have not made any mistakes.

Sign the letter at the bottom clearly, and print your name beneath your signature.

If there are only a few applicants for the job, the prospective employer will probably interview all of them. However, when there are a large number then he will 'weed' out the unsuitable ones just by looking at the letters. Your letter is, therefore, a vital part of getting an interview at all.

It is no use saying that you are 'applying for the job you have advertised'. You need to say just what job it is.

Say when you are available for interview, as it may cause some embarrassment if they ask you to attend at an inconvenient time.

Will it really suit me?

Before you send the application off, make sure that you *really want* the job that you are applying for. You must have read carefully the advertisement or description of the job and you should already have talked it over with a person in a position to advise you.

Put this practical question to yourself: suppose the outcome of my application was favourable, would I have any doubt about accepting the offer?

If you appear to have any doubts at all at the interview, then this would prejudice the whole thing. You must have thought it through beforehand and arrive at the interview determined that you do want the job. Any half-heartedness may spoil your chances.

There is, nevertheless, a problem here that you may have to face. Suppose you have two or three applications out, and are called for interview for the one you regard the least favourably. What do you do? Take them into your confidence and say that if one of the others turns up you will accept it? (If you do, you risk being told not to bother to come.) Or ask for the interview to be postponed, hoping that you will hear good news from one of the others. (You *might* be lucky, but don't count on it.) Or go to the interview and accept the offer if it is made, with a mental reservation to cancel it if a better offer comes from elsewhere? (This is sometimes done, and you may regard it as a risk that people making appointments have to accept. How would you like it, though, if you were offered and accepted a place only to have the offer withdrawn later? In the last resort, only you can decide what to do when your interests and your sense of fairness pull different ways.)

Application forms

In many instances, you apply for a job by filling in an application form rather than by writing a letter on your own initiative. Here is a check list of questions which you should ask yourself:

Have I filled in the application fully and accurately?
Are there any mis-spellings or faults of expression?

If there are likely to be any of these, it is best to get a friend to look over a rough draft beforehand.

Is the handwriting easy to read?

This is not a trivial question. Your application is an important document. You need to keep the reader on your side.

Are there any omissions to fill in, or revisions to make?

There shouldn't be any if you gave proper attention to your rough draft. If you need to alter, do so boldly. Don't spoil the appearance of the application with smudged deletions or scrawled additions.

The most important part of your application form is almost certainly the part in which you are free to write your own description of your career, interests, and supporting material.

Is this description in logical order?
Does it say all you want to say? And does it say it in a clear, fluent style, not breathlessly enthusiastic on the one hand, or terse and off-putting on the other?

Has it got any obvious omissions that will lead the reader to guess what you have left out, perhaps to your disadvantage?

Does it give most space to the important things, and less to the smaller details?

Have you used fully the space provided? If not, your interviewer will have to draw out further facts when he meets you, and he may feel that you have wasted some of his time in not setting them down in the first place.

Have you gone on to a further sheet if the application form invited you to do this? If so, make sure that the information on this sheet carries due weight; it is just as bad to be garrulous on paper as in conversation.

Sometimes you are expected to set out the whole of your application in your own way. This is a useful exercise in

SCHOOL leaver required for labouring or to learn bricklaying.

YOUNG PERSON wanted for clerical work. Training will be given but applicant must be interested in the motor trade.—Apply in writing to the Service Manager.

WORKING Cook-Housekeeper required by professional man and wife. Own self-contained bed-sitting room and bath.—Write or telephone.

PLANT FINANCE—REGIONAL MANAGERS

Expansion of this specialised finance company necessitates the recruitment of four additional regional managers to develop territories in the United Kingdom.

If you
- ★ are 25 to 35
- ★ successful in selling hire purchase and leasing
- ★ frustrated by having a multiplicity of services to sell
- ★ prefer dealing with industrial business at top level
- ★ are not content with a routine nine till five existence
- ★ are looking for bigger opportunities than your present company can offer

We can offer
- ★ unique chance to contribute to the growth of a national finance company not yet two years old.
- ★ hard work
- ★ the chance of joining a young and aggressive management team
- ★ a quality company car
- ★ an excellent salary

Interested?
Write in the first instance giving details of career to date

HAIRDRESSING. Ladies' stylist or improver required, must be interested in long hair or willing to learn. School leaver also required, 5 day week, Saturday half day, good wages and commission.

We have vacancy for young person with minimum of 2 A level passes who is interested in a worthwhile career in which full training is given. — Please apply for interview to Branch Manager.

SECRETARY (Shorthand not essential). Interesting and absorbing work dealing with people and situations in central office on London Road. The position requires a person of exceptional personality, good telephone manner and who can work on own initiative.

Among our most highly paid employees are many people who come to us well qualified in a completely different field from ours. With us they have no limit. For a preliminary discussion send details of age (25–43), education and experience to:

LEFT SCHOOL OR COLLEGE AND UNDECIDED WHAT TO DO?

We don't expect any young person to finally decide on the future before 25, that is why our training scheme for Junior Sales Executives is designed to give a thorough grounding in the operation of a modern, international manufacturing sales organisation, initially, with a strong bias towards Direct Selling to industry.

Salary commencing at up to £xxxx per annum (depending on age) with the chance to earn early increases. There are excellent opportunities for advancement into Field Sales and management at home or in South Africa, Canada, Australia and U.S.A.

Young people aged up to 23 should write or telephone for further details, quoting reference 2009.

TELEPHONIST

Person aged 21–40, required for National Daily Newspaper G.P.O. trained pref. thoroughly experienced 1A lamp signalling board. £xx per week.

MACHINE ROOM MANAGER.

We are looking for a progressive Machine Room Manager to take full control of department in the Letterpress/small Litho Field. Applicants should be completely technical and have had previous control of running a department. Please write or phone.

ARE YOU AN EXPERIENCED GENERAL FOREMAN?

A GENERAL FOREMAN

(two posts) required to assist Site Supervisor in controlling contract for erection of Council flats due to start in near future. Must have proven ability in this work and of handling all trades. Salary based on 40-hour week. Overtime as directed.

Appointment for duration of contract. Salary scale £xxxx to £xxxx.

INSURANCE CO. requires person age up to 30 years, experience in all aspects of Motor Claims to assist Head Office Motor Claims Superintendent in overseeing Branch handling. The post offers a secure and progressive career. A generous salary, LVs and non-contributory Pension Scheme in respect of which consideration will be given to previous Insurance service.

A YOUNG PERSON with experience of order routine and some knowledge of paper and costing, required for internal printing department. Excellent conditions with assurance, pension and sickness scheme.

INVOICE CLERKS (either sex). Experienced invoice clerk, preferably with travel agency experience, required end November for charge of invoice section of foreign touring office. Salary to £xxxx p.a. for the right person. Pension scheme. Also juniors. 19 plus, from £xx p.w., L.Vs.

We are a leading company in the field of specialised packaging products. Continuing expansion and diversification call for the appointment of a top-calibre person to the newly created position of Regional Sales Manager (South).

Experience of leading a small industrial sales team, together with the ability to negotiate at senior management level are essential requirements. A knowledge of the paper and/or packaging industries, while not essential, would be a distinct advantage. The successful candidate will be aged 30–45, and will preferably reside within easy access of Slough.

Commencing salary £xxxx plus bonus. Group contributory pension and life assurance schemes operate, and a company car is provided.

Write in confidence, with full personal and career details to the Sales Director.

organizing clear, brief, factual statements. Set the facts out boldly, spacing them well, and underlining the headings. Your written application is your shop window. Dress it carefully, and don't be too modest about it!

You will find more information about application forms in 'How to prepare your application' (p. 66).

Answering advertisements

These advertisements form a representative sample of what you might see among others in the 'small ad'. SITUATIONS VACANT column of your local newspaper, together with some 'display ads.' of a similar type.

One or two of them invite you to send for details of the vacancies. In these cases you should do this before you send in a formal application or ask for an interview. When you send for details there is no need to say anything at all about yourself. You can make the request in a single sentence.

For example:

(Your address)
(Date)

Recruiting Officer,
OS/Typing,
Dept. of the Environment.

Dear Sir,
Please send me details of your vacancies for Junior Copy Typists.

Yours faithfully,
(Your name)

In this case there is no need, either, to send a stamped, addressed envelope.

When advertisers invite applications from people who are qualified ('experienced', 'fully experienced', 'skilled', 'capable', 'first class') a list of exams passed, and relevant experience gained, must be given. But they often ask for other, and more general, qualities, such as 'intelligent', 'of good personality', 'with drive', 'responsible', etc. These are useful in telling the candidate the kind of questions that the employer might ask about him of a head teacher or other referee. There is nothing the candidate can do about them at the stage of seeking an interview, but he can be sure that he will be expected to give examples of drive and of responsibilities he has undertaken at the interview itself.

When you can offer an employer something which is not vital, but is a useful extra, it is worth mentioning this in your c.v. or preliminary letter, in case the letters at this stage are used to sift out the candidates. If you have been attracted by an advertisement which says 'some audio experience would be useful', or 'typing an advantage', or 'shorthand knowledge an asset', and you can offer something towards this 'extra', tell them so.

If the advertisement refers to training, express your willingness to accept this, but don't make a long story of it. An interviewer will often open his conversation with a candidate by referring to points made in the candidate's letter. A candidate would set out on the right foot if his interviewer began 'From your letter you seem keen to start training . . .'

Sample Letters

A brief, fairly basic letter, asking for an interview for work in a general office, might be:

(Your address)
(Date)

Office Manager.

Dear Sir,

I am 16 years of age, and am due to leave Hillside Comprehensive School at the end of the summer term. I wish to apply for the vacancy in your general office advertised in last night's Leicester Mercury.

I can come for interview at any time out of school hours, or perhaps within school hours by arrangement with the Headmaster. I enclose some details about myself.

Yours faithfully,
(Your name)

A fuller letter, in reply to this advertisement

> **We have a vacancy for young person with minimum of 2 A level passes who is interested in a worthwhile career in which full training is given. Please apply for interview to Branch Manager.**

might take the following lines, if you were not sending a c.v.

(Your address)
(Date)

Branch Manager.

Dear Sir,

I am interested in the vacancy you advertise for a young person with a minimum of 2 A-levels.

I am 18 years of age, and am due to leave Shepstead 6th-Form College at the end of the Summer term. I already have 5 O-levels and one A-level, and am waiting to hear the result of two further A-levels, one of which is in Mathematics, which I have a reasonable expectation of passing.

I have talked about a career in insurance with my uncle, who is an agent with an insurance company.

I am available for interview at any time, except for the week beginning June 26th, when I shall be engaged on a survey with a group from the school. You can contact me at home by telephone, if you wish. Our number is ...

If you would like any further details about me before the interview, the Headmaster will be prepared to give them.

Yours faithfully,
(Your name)

Most straightforward jobs for those who leave school as soon as possible after they have reached school-leaving age are filled by personal application, either by turning up within the hours given in the advertisement, or by an appointment arranged over the telephone.

Some prospective employers may use the telephone conversation to make a preliminary assessment of you. Be ready. Think it out before you call. Be positive on the telephone and don't mumble. Know your qualifications and be sure you are really interested in the job. Otherwise you may find they tell you not to bother to come, particularly if they are trying to sift out those applicants for whom an interview would be a waste of time.

Such jobs might be advertised as follows:

'The Handyman' requires young person, aged 16–20 years, to train in the sales department, clean and tidy appearance, good prospect of advancement. Apply to ...

Grandisons require full-time assistant. Apply to ...

As soon as you read advertisements like these in your local newspaper, you can probably picture the shops concerned, and have perhaps been inside as a customer. The second of the advertisements is very uninformative indeed, and it would certainly pay you to visit the premises before you thought seriously about applying. (What is the range of articles they sell? Does the shop give a good impression? Presumably they don't mind whether a boy or girl applies for the job, but which would have the better chance?, etc.)

'The Handyman' premises would be worth a visit too (unless you know them very well). Does the shop live up to the kind of salesman they hope to get? You might decide that it does, and be sufficiently attracted to apply.

Smaller firms would most commonly expect you to 'phone up to arrange a time for an interview, and you should do so as soon as you can after spotting the advertisement, otherwise the job may be gone! However, if it was a weekend or evening you might make a good impression by writing a letter like the one below and putting it through the letterbox:–

(Your address)
(Date)

'The Handyman'

Dear Sir,
I wish to apply for training as salesman in your shop.
I am 16 years of age, and have just left ... School. I
think I can truthfully say that I am smart in appearance.
I think, too, that I would make a good salesman. I
have sometimes helped out in a general stores run by a
friend of the family, and I have sold programmes,
tickets, etc., for charities and various school events.
At school, I was in the top half of my class in most
subjects, and passed in three C.S.E. subjects.
I played regularly for the school in the Association
Football League, and for my House at football and
other sports.
In my last year at school I was a prefect, and carried
out some duties in the library. I have made many things
in the school workshops, and have helped to construct
scenery for school plays. I have also done some do-it-
yourself jobs at home.
I am available at any time, and look forward to
hearing from you.

Yours faithfully,
(Your name)

This is not a long letter, but it is long enough to help the
shop owner to make up his mind whether or not he would
like to interview the writer. The young man has at least
shown a practical interest in the two vital matters: selling,
and being a handyman.
Need he have mentioned exam successes and his position
in the class? Emphatically, yes. Rightly or wrongly, success
in exams provides a stamp of quality in most employers'
eyes. Probably rightly, because even in a practical situation
like selling in a handyman's shop, academic successes prove
that the applicant possesses versatility and personal resource
that may be useful in many (and perhaps unexpected) ways.

Similarly, in an application for a 'bookish' job, success at sport or in a leisure pursuit proves that the candidate has a width of interest that may help him to adapt to changing circumstances in his job. In the course of time, jobs are bound to change, and the only kind of worker who is worth employing up to retirement is one who can cope with changes as they come.

As an example of an application for a 'bookish' job we might take a nationally-advertised vacancy in a Borough Treasurer's Department:

JUNIOR CLERK
Applicants with at least 3 GCE 'O' levels are invited for the above post which has excellent career prospects.

Borough Treasurer.

(Your address)
(Date)

Dear Sir,

I should be glad to be considered for the post of Junior Clerk in your Department.

I am 16, and have just left ... School. The following are my GCE subjects and grades: (There follows a neat table).

I took other, non-examination subjects as well, and was particularly interested in a General Course which included Social Studies.

I played a full part in school life, and have been Prefect, House Captain, and a regular member of the football and cricket teams. One of my proudest possessions is the bronze award of the Duke of Edinburgh's scheme. I am a strong swimmer, and have gained life saving and swimming certificates.

In my spare time, I am a motor cycle enthusiast, and a do-it-yourselfer. I also read a lot, and have contributed articles to the school magazine.

I am free to come for interview at any time.

Yours faithfully,
(Your name)

Personal application

Most school leavers continue to live at home when they take their first job, so they naturally look for work a convenient travelling distance away. Since the work is near, it is equally natural for them to look the place over before they actually apply. When the advertisements say 'inquire', 'apply to', or even 'write or telephone', why not call?

You might be seen on the spot by the person in charge of filling the vacancy (though you would be lucky if this happened), but at least you could make arrangements for an interview.

Personal application, if you are successful in being seen at once, has the advantage of cutting down the period of waiting and worrying. If you are not seen on the spot, at least you have got a little of the 'feel' of the place. This is important, because so much of the anxiety of being interviewed is due to fear (if this is not too strong a term) of the unknown. The more you can learn beforehand, the less the unknown can worry you.

Do I really want them?

One particular feature that you will be able to satisfy yourself about is the size of the concern. This may be mentioned in the advertisement itself ('a small company', for example, or 'a member of the ... group of companies').

A small concern often has a happy, family atmosphere, in which everybody knows everybody else, and all are concerned with each other's welfare. Close contact between employer and employees may make for friendliness and reasonable efficiency. On the other hand, for the ambitious young worker, progress up the ladder may be blocked. A larger concern may have a good atmosphere too. The responsibilities and duties in it are likely to be more clear cut, and the ladder of promotion more open (and longer, too).

The size of the place you work in, like all the other features you look for, depends, in the end, on your personal preference, and, of course, on the availability of the kind of work you want.

One thing to avoid in a preliminary letter is asking those questions which should wait for the interview itself. This underlines the need, in your own interests, to go as well prepared as possible to interview.

Put very simply: the interview is the last occasion on which you are on anything approaching equal terms with your prospective employer. If you don't like him, or his firm, you can say 'no' and depart gracefully. But it is less easy to haggle when he is the employer and you the employee. Find out at interview, then, just what the advertisement meant when it said

> 'This position offers scope for advancement to a conscientious worker'

or, 'Good salary for hard worker'

or, 'Good pay and conditions'

or, 'Proficiency payments'

or, 'Full training'
> etc.

The school leaver will want to know 'When do I start?' but he should also go to interview with some idea about when he is prepared to start. He will need a holiday between finishing at school and starting work.

Do they mean Me?

When you read an advertisement for a job, take careful note of what the advertiser wants. Advertisements cost money, so an employer isn't going to pad out his description of a job with unnecessary words.

If, for example, you are attracted by an advertisement which calls for someone who is 'able to work without supervision', it is no use making an application which omits any reference to work which you have done on your own. At interview, you are bound to be asked about worthwhile work done either on your own initiative or with minimum guidance. You should go ready with samples of such work, which could be some do-it-yourself at home, a project at school, or a youth club venture in which your contribution fitted in with what other members did, or a hobby you have pursued.

Asked about work done without supervision, you might, in the course of conversation, say something like this: 'I can stick at a job until it's finished. I don't need to go running to someone else every five minutes to know how to go on. I find my own way round most problems, unless I can see that I'm wasting my time, or spoiling material, or something like that. Of course, I have to make sure I understand what's wanted in the first place, but once I've been shown, I pick it up pretty quickly'.

This sounds very well, but an employer may wonder whether you stick at a job you set yourself, but wouldn't be wholehearted about one set by an employer. Some tasks are demanding and repetitive ones outside an applicant's personal interests. (One remedy for this lies with the employer: to see that work is as far as possible varied enough not to be an insult to a lively person's skill and intelligence.) An employer's doubts may be set at rest by examples of corporate effort, where the applicant has worked on his own to contribute to something that others have had a share in making too.

You can't make a long story of this in a written application, but a reference to work without supervision is worth a couple of sentences, or so. For example:

'In my last year at school I have done a number of things with little or no supervision. These include canvassing for advertisements for our school magazine, preparing models for demonstration at our annual exhibition, and the production of a folder on transport in our town for C.S.E. exam'.

Personal relationships are another common theme in 'Situations Vacant' advertisements. Here is one of the variations: 'Able to deal with customer contact by letter and telephone'.

You might be able to say to your interviewer: 'I get on well with people, and have enough patience to hear them out. I catch on pretty quickly to what they are telling me, and can answer them briefly and to the point. I took a part-time job in a local store during the last summer holidays, and I think I served the public as cheerfully and efficiently as the full-time staff'.

In a written application there would be no need to refer to letter-writing because the application itself takes the form of a letter, but it would be useful if you could say 'I speak clearly, and my friends tell me that I have a good telephone manner'. When you write about your part-time job you might be able to mention that it involved some telephoning, even if it was only on an internal line. At least it would show acquaintance with the instrument.

The 'cryptic' advertiser
Some advertisers have a clear idea of their vacancies and of the people they hope will fill them, but the advertisements they publish are deliberately cryptic. What do you make of this?

'Are you a young person 16–18 looking for employment? Then perhaps you would like to train for a
specific job of an interesting nature with prospects'.

No other details are given, except for an address, a
telephone number, and the office hours during which you
may make your inquiries.

Employment agencies may advertise in this rather vague
way, and so, sometimes, may firms with a number of
openings, who hope that young people, attracted by
curiosity, and by the words 'interesting', 'prospects' (or
whatever other words are used) will apply.

Applicants risk wasting their time on these uninformative
advertisements, but they may, on the other hand, gain from
turning up at a place they wouldn't otherwise have
considered for a job, to discover that the work, conditions,
and atmosphere there are all just what they want. This
underlines the fact that in job-hunting nothing can take the
place of on-the-spot inquiry.

In the Waiting Room

You are almost certain to spend some time waiting, partly because some interviewers seem to delight in keeping people hanging around, but more importantly because:-

YOU HAVE GOT TO ARRIVE IN GOOD TIME

Under no circumstances must you be late. After all a candidate who can't even manage to get to the interview on time is hardly likely to be a good time-keeper if he is given the job.

There is one problem you share with your interviewer: that of appearing bright and fresh at the start of the interview.

Whether this meeting with you is first or last on his list, you will expect your interviewer to be considerate in putting his questions and patient in hearing your answers.

You would be surprised, and annoyed, if others before you had worn him down, and so irritated him that he seemed anxious only to be rid of you.

You will find your session in the waiting room as wearing as he finds a succession of interviewees. As a rule, interviews are timed so that the waiting period is short. Even so, long waits are common and often harassing.

If you are waiting alone, the lack of human support may bring on a fit of nerves. If others are waiting with you, you may be shattered by their apparent confidence, their gossip – which always somehow suggests that they are 'in the know' and that you are an outsider – and their vast fund of experience.

Take it all with a pinch of salt. Others are as nervous as you are. Their 'confidence' may cover up a gnawing uncertainty. They may look assured because they are better actors than you are. Their chatter, and the experiences they exchange, may be a defence mechanism. They may fear drying up in the interview room, or stumbling in their speech, or saying foolish things, so they need to prove to themselves beforehand that they aren't like this at all.

Besides, what makes you think that nerves are a bad thing? They have a very useful function to perform – so long as you don't let them get on top of you. They are nature's way of mobilizing your resources for what is to come.

Sometimes, candidates wait gloomily with nothing said but the barest courtesies. If this is the situation you find when you are ushered in, you might as well conform. Any brightness you attempt will probably sound dreadfully hollow (though it is conceivable that the others may be grateful to you for livening things up).

Preliminary thoughts

The best preliminary to your interview is to keep your mind active. You don't want to go in looking and feeling so inert that it takes all the interviewer's skill to rouse you. Keep yourself alert by running over some of the points you expect to come up in the space of your interview. (But don't worry at one particular point so long that you will be put off if the interview takes an unexpected turn and it doesn't come up at all.)

A quick round-up of points for the interview ensures that when your questioner raises them they will be in your recent memory, and you won't have to sit there tongue-tied while you try to dredge them up from the more distant past.

You might try to frame for yourself the kind of questions which will trigger the points off. Keep the questions simple, and your answers too.

Don't attempt to learn up answers to likely questions. If you do, you will probably produce a horrible, stilted, rehearsed effect. The facts, ideas, and comments you express are more important than the words in which you clothe them. Trust yourself, therefore, and follow the maxim: 'Take care of the sense, and the sounds will take care of themselves.'

Don't worry about the others

If the door to the interview room is solid and forbidding,

and you can't hear a squeak of what is happening on the other side of it, don't let your imagination worry you sick with the idea that the candidate before you is getting a grilling, and that you will shortly be getting one too. Occupy yourself more profitably with your review of interview points.

Sometimes, though, you can hear the occasional burst of shared laughter from the room, or the soothing sound of normal conversation. This should put heart into you.

What are you to make of the candidates passing through the waiting room after their interview?

You will probably be reassured by their everyday appearance. They won't look as if they've had a shattering experience – and nor will you when your interview is over. You may even get from one of them the wink which says that the interviewer has proved unexpectedly human, and that the whole business wasn't so bad after all.

Even if a candidate comes out looking unwontedly thoughtful, it probably only means that he had a question he meant to ask but when the opportunity came he couldn't for the life of him think what it was. It often happens that you only think of the really important questions when you've got outside the door.

What makes a Good Interview?

A good interview will achieve 'rapport' between interviewer and candidate. They will find common ground, and go over it in a congenial atmosphere.

The candidate will leave the room with the feeling that he did himself justice, that he had ample opportunity to show his quality, and that his interviewer appreciated and approved that quality.

Even if, in the end, the candidate is turned down, he will have sufficient confidence in his interviewer to feel sure that the successful candidate must have deserved his success.

The interviewer, on his side, will feel that he has got the best out of each candidate, and probed deeply enough to make a decision that will stand the test of experience.

Everything depends on mutual trust. It is safe to say that your interviewer, whoever he is, regards himself as an open-minded, friendly person, anxious to give you the chance to show your paces. He is looking for the best possible candidate, and you may turn out to be the one who fits this description exactly.

You may gather a rather different impression of him. You may see him as self-important, and so ready to let fly with his opinions and criticism that he doesn't give you a chance. The very worst you could think of him is that the interview he conducted was a charade: that it was a foregone conclusion and that he never intended to accept you. (Sometimes this impression is due to listening too avidly to waiting-room gossip, and going into the interview convinced that the place was already promised to someone else. This could be part of the mythology of interviews, fostered so that disappointed candidates can put the blame for a poor performance on the interviewer rather than themselves.)

It is no use entering the interview room in a frame of mind that guarantees frustration for you. (Even if your interviewer is as bad as the worst you can think of him, you will at least gain useful experience, and your attitude to the situation may lead him to see merit in you that he did not expect.)

In a situation that you cannot control, the best thing you can do is to trust your interviewer, who might turn out less formidable than you expected. Your trust will nearly always be well placed. If you have prepared yourself properly for the experience (or ordeal, if you think of it that way) you will almost certainly be able to cope with whatever turns up.

There is one respect in which you may unwittingly do your interviewer an injustice. He is likely to receive you with cordiality to give you confidence and to get things moving smoothly. His manner, and the patient hearing he gives you, may suggest that he looks with special favour on your application. 'We got on like a house on fire!' might be your reaction.

But suppose you are rejected after all. Is your further reaction to be 'The two-faced so-and-so!'?

It shouldn't be. His cordiality is the same for others as for you. It is part of his style. Don't misinterpret it and end by thinking him a hypocrite.

Equally, if you are accepted, it is clear that you did a persuasive public relations job for yourself in convincing him of your merit. But don't imagine that his friendly manner might have told you that already. Interviewers don't give themselves away as easily as that.

Presenting Yourself

An interviewer nearly always has an interview sheet to fill in. He has it spread in front of him, and usually completes it unobtrusively. (You may find it rather daunting if he fills in the sheet about you with relish, or heavy breathing, or with much taking up and putting down of writing materials. Don't be too dismayed. He hasn't singled you out. He's like this with everyone, and if you keep your nerve your composure may lead him to write something to your credit. He might be doing this anyway.)

He probably has a line to complete on your appearance. What would you like him to put?

It's just as well to take stock well beforehand, and ask yourself what impression you want to create. Ask yourself, too, what impression you think you *do* create.

An interview is an important occasion – and not only for you. It is reasonable to expect candidates to be dressed appropriately. (One candidate turned up to an interview leading to professional training wearing rather rough working clothes. He defended his dress by saying that he wanted the interviewer to see him as he really was, and not dressed for the occasion. His attitude was laudable, no doubt, and his interviewer was duly glad that he had seen him 'as he really was'.)

Most candidates come to interview dressed in their best. I know that an interview is an artificial situation, and that when candidates dress up for it (and perhaps put on extra manners too, and make tongue-in-cheek claims about themselves and their experiences) the interviewer may have little idea of what they are like in a more everyday situation. But at least he knows that they are prepared to put themselves out in a situation of importance. An interviewer may deduce that if candidates are casual in dress they are probably casual in other things too. Correspondingly, if they take care of their appearance they may be just the careful people he is looking for.

A practical way of looking at how you should dress is this. Suppose you were successful at interview, how would you dress in the situation to which your application leads? Dress for interview so as to look the part. A professional man should look like a professional man, a supervisor like a supervisor, etc. If you don't look the part, how can you expect people to take you seriously?

We all know that people of equal status, or in the same occupation, don't all dress alike. There must be some individuality too. This is where your temperament and taste come in. Do you want to stand out, or fit in? Are you a bit of an introvert, keeping yourself to yourself, and preferring to merge into the background rather than seek publicity? Either way, you can dress acceptably and still create the right image. If you are in any doubt at all, dress quietly and tidily so that you don't draw too much attention to yourself.

It may help you to look over this alphabetical list of words and phrases. Which would you like to be written against 'Appearance' on *your* interview sheet? Would it worry you if any of the others were used to describe you?

Colourless	Smart
Drab	Soberly dressed
Dressed in working clothes	Unkempt
Dressed to kill	Untidy
Fashionably dressed	Up-to-the-minute
Gimmicky	Well groomed
Neat	With-it
Over-dressed	
Presentable	

What gets written as a rule is factual and descriptive, but some terms imply criticism. Once it is written down, a critical description stands against you. You are not in a position to look over the interviewer's shoulder to see what he has put, so you are unable to defend yourself if you sense a bit of hostility.

Sometimes an interviewer will raise a question of appearance with a candidate:

'Is your hair always as long as this?'
'Weren't you able to tidy yourself up?'
'Have you come here straight from work?'
'I notice you bite your fingernails. Has this always been a habit of yours?'

He won't want to dwell on any of these things – and nor will you – but they help fill in the picture for him.

Structuring the Interview

No interview is exactly like any other. This is because no candidate is like any other.

An interview must be adaptable enough to meet the special needs of every interviewee, whoever he is. Yet it needn't be an aimless, gossipy chat. It has a serious purpose, and this can't be achieved unless there is a basic structure. Otherwise, comparisons could not properly be made, and the competitive element which is built into so many interviews would be plainly unfair.

The interviewer must ask all the questions necessary to form a rounded picture of each candidate, and to some extent these must be standardized. If the interview were too slavishly standardized, the information might just as well be got by means of a questionnaire (in this case, an extremely detailed application form).

An interview is really a compromise between a structured, standardized, the-same-for-all inquiry, and an open-ended conversation which is allowed to develop along lines basically dictated by the candidate himself. An interview which attempts to do justice to the candidate (and, don't forget, the needs of the organization to which he is applying) will start as the one and end as the other.

It doesn't follow that the interviewer gradually loses control. His role is to seek conclusions and to prevent drift. This is as much in the candidate's interest as his own. If the interview were allowed to fizzle out, both parties would share a dissatisfied feeling that the whole affair got nowhere, and the candidate would know that he had failed.

There is only one remedy for this situation: preparation by the candidate in presenting his case. He mustn't flop when the point arrives when the interviewer in effect says 'Over to you'.

How to Give the Right Impression

Don't count on your interviewer learning, by question and answer, all that he ought to know about you before he can make his decision. Make up your mind beforehand what, in your own interests, you want to tell him.

This extra information is vital. It rounds off your interviewer's total impression of you, and this is of greater importance than the skills that 'go with the job'. (What use would it be appointing a young person to help with the books simply because he was good at mathematics, if he was also dishonest, or a frequent absentee?) If the will to learn is there, the skills can be acquired with experience, but attitudes and outlooks can't be so easily changed. A young person might quite easily get taken on with less than the qualifications asked for if the interviewing employer feels 'I like the look of him', or 'He's a person after my own heart', or 'He's got something about him'.

Just what you've got about you may not be brought out in a conversation about the job unless you come prepared to express yourself.

A prospective employer (i.e. an employer from whom you are seeking a job) is bound to be interested in why you are applying for work in his particular field:

How long have you thought of taking up this kind of work?
Is your father (or brother, or any other relation) in a similar line?
Have you any friends doing this kind of work?
Do you know anyone who is working in the firm?

(A very useful pointer this; it suggests that you have talked it over with him, and that you already feel positively attracted by the work, or the firm, or both. It is also a useful pointer when two friends who have left school together seek work together, though employers are sometimes cautious about this; friends in jobs can waste each other's time. I have heard a builder declare 'When you have an apprentice, you have an apprentice. If you have two apprentices, you have half an apprentice. If you have three apprentices, you have no apprentice'. Do you see what he means?)

Why did you apply to work with us?

(If there are a number of openings in the locality it is interesting to an employer to know why you picked on him. Was it simply because his place of work is nearest to your home? Or because of his reputation as an employer? Or because he offers a good service or product to the public? Or did you apply to him because you hadn't bothered to find out what openings there were elsewhere? On the other hand, did you apply because of some personal recommendation you had? This last is, naturally, a strong card to play.)

Is this kind of work your first choice (or would you rather have done something else, and your hopes have been dashed)?

(It is obviously more attractive to an employer to take on someone who has chosen his kind of work in preference to any other. If the work comes a poor second to what the young worker really wants, the employer may fear that he may drift away if something apparently more attractive turns up. If you can say that the work you are applying for is genuinely what you want, this is clearly in your favour.

Some young people haven't a very realistic idea of what jobs are possible for them, and they may dream of 'glamour jobs'. A boy may be mad keen on football, but lack the talent that will turn him into the professional he would like to be. A girl may not have the figure or the poise to be a TV star or an air hostess. Commonsense in the end comes to the rescue of nearly all young people who live in a romantic dream-world, but an employer may notice what he thinks is a poor attitude in a boy or girl when the real cause is a sense of let-down, because the job hasn't the glamour he or she had hoped for.)

What have you done?

Your prospective employer will be interested to hear what subjects you did at school, how successful you were at them, and which subjects you were really interested in. It will be much in your favour if your most successful, or your favourite, subjects lead naturally towards the kind of employment he can offer you. He may need to see proofs of success or achievement that you claim, in the shape of exam certificates or school reports. Have them ready in case he wants to see them.

A question at the back of your prospective employer's mind, though he may not ask it in this form (and perhaps he will not ask it at all) is this: 'What have you done at school, or in your spare time, that would help to convince me that you are the person I'm looking for? Can you give me any evidence to back up your application?'

Certificates and testimonials are one kind of evidence, and testimonials, although regarded with suspicion by some interviewers, are often important at the start of working life when you cannot demonstrate much experience. You may be able to use them to demonstrate application.

If you are a practical person, looking for a practical job, then bring along evidence of things you have made, or planned, and carried out yourself. Some things can't be brought along, of course (for example, the fitment built into a room of your house), but a photo, accurate drawing, or sketch will show what you have done. Useful articles made in wood, metal, or other materials are a good guide to skill and interest. These may range from serviceable do-it-yourself to examples of genuine craftsmanship. The artistic is often as good a guide as the useful. I have seen paintings, pottery, musical instruments, dress designs, and many other things produced at interview. One effect of showing a wider range of things at interview is to prove that a boy who is 'good with his hands' is not necessarily lacking in ideas or imagination too – and the same goes for the girl.

What is the interview really for?

Never forget that an interview is not just a conversation about work between an employer and a prospective employee. All the time the conversation is going on, the employer is trying to picture the applicant in the job they are talking about.

When you come up for interview, the employer will have this advantage (among others) over you: he knows all the duties that go with the job, and all the demands it would make on you, if he appointed you. How can you convince him that you could cope with it?

There are several answers to this question.

You wouldn't have applied in the first place if you hadn't some idea what the work entails, and could picture yourself doing it. You know whether it needs strength, or some physical skill that you possess and could develop, or good eyesight and attention to detail, or the capacity to stand doing repetitive movements; you know whether it is indoors or out, and whether it involves travel; you know, too, whether it involves meeting people, particularly the public.

A job that needs strength or stamina calls for a good health record, in which case you will be ready with details of health and things you have done that prove your fitness. For a job that calls for mechanical sense you will need to show your acquaintance with machinery, perhaps through driving, or car or motor cycle repair and maintenance.

Work in a shop will include duties which must be done with care, courtesy, and accuracy. Can you handle goods without being clumsy? Can you listen patiently to a member of the public explaining what she wants, and help her to find it, or perhaps a near alternative, in the shop? Could you take money and give change throughout a day and be able to account for it all at the end? Can you take orders from a superior, even if you don't always see the point of them?

Does your experience in school, at home, or in a shop as a customer, throw any light on how you would take to shop work? If so, speak out at your interview.

Work as a secretary or receptionist demands neatness and good organization, and the capacity to write or type businesslike letters and to use the telephone. Can you do all these things? If you made a written application, you certainly proved whether you can write a good letter, but what about the other things? I have known a girl with quite a lot to commend her lose the chance of a secretarial job because her prospective employer asked himself at her interview 'What would a member of the public make of her at the other end of a telephone line?'

If applicants lack the physical or technical skills necessary for a job, they simply don't put in for it. They know from their health or sports record at school, or from poor exam results what they are lacking, and they can't very well deceive themselves that they possess what is wanted.

Try a bit of self-criticism

But social skills aren't examined or tested in the same way, so there is plenty of scope for an applicant to put in for a job that really wouldn't suit. He (or she) must test himself for smartness (if this is called for in a job), or the ability to meet members of the public in a helpful and relaxed way, or the ability to write a letter of information, advice, or complaint, or the ability to use a phone. If you can't be self-critical, you are not yet ready to put in an application which an employer can take seriously.

Self-criticism is all very well, but what are you to do about the failings you see in yourself? On the way you present yourself, for example. There are plenty of newspapers and magazines (as well as parents and friends) free with advice on good grooming and dressing well. The important thing is to choose a style which suits yourself, and unless you are very discriminating you may need to seek a friend's helpful opinion.

Many young people dress smartly, yet give themselves

away when they open their mouths. This is not to suggest that you, as a candidate for a job, have got to speak with a put-on BBC accent, but that you drop any rough, slangy speech that may go down well enough among friends, and make a conscious effort to speak clearly in an adult way.

If your job calls for meeting the public, why not visit shops, showrooms, and other places where salespeople and officials actually meet the public, and exercise your capacity for appreciation and criticism on what you see and hear? Who, among those you observe, would you like to model yourself on? Who is an 'awful warning'?

The courtesy, patience, tolerance, ability to listen, and other qualities shown by people on the job already will also be expected of you. If you can learn to suppress faults in yourself in time for your first meeting with your prospective employer, and can bring out the personal relationships you can already manage quite well, you are likely to do better than the candidate who comes along hoping to 'play it all by ear'.

As for using a telephone, and sound like a responsible adult to the person at the other end of the line, there is only one recipe for success, and that is experience. Learn the routine of making a call and ring up a friend. (Find out the cost of a call beforehand, and bear in mind who is paying.) What is your friend's candid opinion of your performance? If your friend is at all critical, is it possible that the same criticisms might apply to your performance at interview? If so, the remedy is obvious – isn't it?

All this is part of the process of helping your prospective employer to picture you in the job for which you are applying. There are other ways too.

Know where you are going

The most convincing way of showing that you are fit for a job is to be able to prove (if you can) that you've already done a similar kind of job in the form of part-time or holiday work.

In this respect, it is an immense advantage to know, well

before you leave school, what kind of full-time work you will eventually seek. This should help you to choose the kind of part-time work that will show whether you have a genuine taste or aptitude for it. Even if your part-time work lies in a different field, it will reveal a lot about yourself, from a simple fact like whether you can get up in time to get to work punctually, to facts like whether you possess the qualities the job demands.

If you can speak with knowledge and enthusiasm about a part-time job you have done successfully, you will have an advantage over an applicant whose capacity to work is an unknown quantity. Moreover, you will be able to use your part-time employer as a referee (with his permission, of course) in applying for full-time employment.

Whatever the job, you will need a period of getting to learn the hang of it. With some jobs, there is a period of training; with others, you learn the job by doing it, under the care of some experienced person. Whether the period of training is long, like an apprenticeship, or short, with a spell under a supervisor before you are on your own, express your willingness and interest in learning to do the job properly. Don't ever make the mistake of turning down offers of help, or give the impression that you think that you know it all from the start.

A good way of expressing your interest, and informing yourself at the same time, is to find out what you can about the firm beforehand. Perhaps you can call and look round. Perhaps you can discover the firm's local reputation and the scope of its activities. Perhaps you can chat with an employee and get an 'inside' view of the job before you really commit yourself to it. (Don't forget, though, that an employee sometimes takes a very prejudiced view of the firm he works for. If he is disgruntled about something you may not be able to take what he says very seriously. If he expresses warm feelings towards his firm this should encourage you. In this case, it would be well to mention it at interview that you know something about the firm already, and that you have spoken to an employee who is very satisfied to work for it.)

Attitudes

However carefully you match what you think a job requires with what you have to offer, there is always something further that you bring to it. You can call this rather grandly your philosophy of life, or you can come down to earth and call it your attitude to work.

The longer your interview, the more surely your attitude will show itself (and the more surely your employer will know whether or not he has picked the right person). If you see work as simply what has to be gone through to provide a wage packet at the end of the week, you are not likely to put your heart into the job. Your prospective employer might then suspect you of being a possible slacker and frequent absentee, and altogether a poor risk.

In fact, though, most people do not put money at the top of the list of what they expect from work. Workpeople – and probably you too – are more likely to put job satisfaction and working among friends at the top of the list.

It is reasonable, though, to look for a combination of things you most value in a job, and it would be a poor interviewer who did not discover something about these things in his conversation with you. You will not be surprised if he draws his own deductions from what he finds out.

Different types of interviewer

If you apply for a job with a small firm, you can expect your interviewer to be shrewd, with an intimate knowledge of the firm's needs. He may be the proprietor himself, or a manager on whom the proprietor relies. He will know, from personal acquaintance, about the careers of others who have served with the firm, and know who turned out to be good appointments, and the few whose appointment turned out to be a mistake. He will know what kind of person the success of the firm depends on, whether that person makes important decisions or simply fits in well with the firm's particular way of doing things. Unless the firm has a fair turnover of staff – a bad sign – an interview will be a fairly rare event.

An interviewer with a large concern (firm, College, local authority, for example) will be kept busier and use methods which are better structured than those used by the small concern. In the technical sense he may well be more 'efficient' but he is likely to have just as many failures as the proprietor of the village shop.

An interview with a small firm is likely to be more chatty and informal than one with a large firm, and you are likely to feel more confident and relaxed because of this, but the need to present yourself well is at least as great in this situation as in the other.

Discussing the terms

One thing almost certain to be discussed is what your pay would be, if appointed. Large Companies and Local Authorities or Government Departments generally have fixed rates of pay which may vary for different grades according to experience, qualifications or assessments. If so, the rate of pay will often have appeared in the advertisement and you would not have applied for the job unless it was acceptable.

With smaller employers the rate of pay may be a matter for negotiation and you should have a clear idea (from friends or even parents) of what to expect – you might even be asked how much you are expecting by the employer! Never expect to get exactly the same wages as your friends – teenage employees should get rises from time to time anyway – but nevertheless if you are offered something well below the going rate, you should be ready to provide chapter and verse examples of pay in similar occupations for people of your own age. No sense in being exploited.

Pay isn't everything. You need to know what else goes with the job. Employment is quite often a 'package deal' with extras thrown in, or inducements offered to the worker to keep down the cost of taking the job. These can be quite substantial; they are also very varied.

Here are some of them: a house that goes with the job; removal expenses to persuade an employee to move to the area of his new work; lodging expenses where the employee has to go away for training; the use of a car (perhaps with private use allowed at week-ends and holidays), or a mileage allowance for the use of the worker's own car; free transport to work and back again; a uniform, or special clothing, or money in lieu; a mid-day meal free to the worker, or subsidized; the right to buy, cheaper than the public can, goods or services produced by the firm; sports facilities, welfare services, etc. 'Perks' include special bonuses or benefits that might be given at Christmas or other times of the year, and the amount of paid holiday that is allowed.

'Perks', in fact, are all those rights which a worker enjoys because he is an employee of a firm or other body. They should be discussed fully at the same time as pay and conditions.

A worker likes to feel that he is looked after by whoever employs him, and correspondingly an employer likes to be regarded as a 'good employer'; in practical terms, this helps to create loyalty among his staff.

It is worth bearing in mind that what seems to the outsider as a very attractive rate of pay sometimes conceals poor conditions of work. (Workers wouldn't accept conditions like that if the pay weren't good.)

When pay seems to be a bit low, so that you might wonder why workers don't drift off into jobs with a bigger pay packet, the explanation may be that 'perks' tip the balance.

In small concerns, the whole 'package' is settled by direct negotiation between employer and employee. The bigger the concern, the more likely it is that pay, conditions, etc., are settled by employers and Trades Unions.

Employers and employees want the best bargain they can make with each other. When the employer offers a particular wage for a job it might not be his last word. Would he pay a higher wage if pressed? What is the prospective employee's bargaining position? What is the bargaining position of someone straight from school who may not know the ins and outs of the labour market?

This last question really answers itself: if a recent school leaver doesn't know the labour situation he isn't in a position to bargain.

Wages depend very much on what is customary in the area. If a newsagent needs another delivery boy, he will expect to pay him what he paid the last one; if a shopkeeper needs an assistant, he will expect to pay the same as he pays other assistants, or what he knows other shopkeepers are paying. When labour of the right sort or quality is scarce, an employer may have to pay higher wages; when there are more workers than jobs, he can recruit them at the usual wages, or even a little less.

People talk, and compare notes, so any changes in the job situation soon become known, and people tend to move off to where pay and conditions are better, unless they have special reasons for staying where they are at the old rates.

Those who have just left school need to discover what rates and conditions are possible in the range of jobs they are willing to undertake. If you are a school leaver, this information will tell you whether or not you are bargaining from a position of strength. It's as well to know!

A SUMMARY OF ADVICE

1. Be ready with all the basic facts about yourself (particularly education, experience, interests, sport, hobbies) that an employer is likely to ask about. Be ready, too, with all the explanations you might be asked to give (the 'how' and 'why' as well as 'what' and 'when'). If you can show that your education, experience, and various activities lead naturally to the kind of employment he has to offer, this is a strong recommendation.

2. Back up your application with tangible evidence if you can, and by referring to any part-time work you have done.

3. Show a genuine interest in the work, and in the firm you have applied to. Part of the proof of this interest is the trouble you have taken to inform yourself about the work and the firm.

4. Try to analyse, as far as you can, the kind of skills and

qualities demanded by the work, and see how far your own skills and qualities match these demands. Apart from training in the work, which you can expect the firm to give, see whether you can discover your own short-comings and remedy them.

5. When you come to interview try to look, speak, and act as the kind of person your prospective employer is looking for. If you can do all this, and still be natural, you will stand a better chance of being accepted. After all, you have left school (or are shortly to leave) and now is your chance to show yourself as a responsible adult.

How to Approach that Test

Candidates for entry into occupations involving practical skill are often asked to undergo a test. This may be anything from a well-established test of aptitude used by a large concern, down to a brief test of know-what and know-how devised and applied by a small employer.

An aptitude test is basically one of practical intelligence. It may test your knowledge, your capacity to 'see through' to the heart of a problem, your ability to understand relationships in a practical setting, the skill of your hands, your observation and attention to detail, your capacity to experiment until you have found the 'right' or the most promising solution, and other qualities bound up with these.

It may include any or all of the following, and more besides:

> 'pencil and paper' tests, rather like intelligence tests and quizzes, but in a practical setting,
> the observation of mechanisms and answering questions about them,
> the assembly of simple mechanisms,
> explanations of how things work,
> the manipulation of wooden blocks, patterned cards, and other test material according to instructions.

These tests may have to be done against the stop-watch.

An aptitude test may include items that might not seem very practical to you, but are designed to discover background knowledge and interests. There is a close tie-up ('correlation') between knowledge, interest, and aptitude.

Aptitude tests reveal qualities which are valuable in a particular kind of job, but they also protect some individuals from undertaking a job they are not really fitted for. It is better to fail such a test, and suffer disappointment before they are committed to the job, than to discover, on the job itself, that they are round pegs in square holes. Aptitude tests are very good at cutting down the number of misfits.

If you have to take an aptitude test, you won't want to throw away your chances by adopting the wrong approach to it.

Commonsense tells you that you should follow all the instructions carefully, and go ahead in a confident and relaxed (but not casual) manner. Experience of tests, however, suggests further, and more detailed advice.

Never under-rate a test, however simple it seems. Every worth-while test has been tried out and checked until we can be sure that there is point and purpose in every item, and that the results given by the test as a whole tally reasonably well with experience.

Easy items help to build confidence and to show the candidate what is expected of him.

I have seen what happens when people scorn the easier items in a graded test, and come in at a later stage, only to find that the later items were harder than they had supposed. Doing the easier items would have helped them to get the hang of the test as a whole.

Don't be worried about failing parts of a test. What would be the point of a test which was so easy that failure was ruled out? It wouldn't really test you at all. Nobody will ever know what you are capable of until you have been brought to the point where you begin to fail.

What interests the tester is where this point comes. What may interest him still more is your attitude to difficulties. Are you easily rattled? Do you keep trying the same wrong approach as if you expect that sheer repetition will turn it into the right one? Have you enough resource to see alternative methods and try them out? Do your attempts suggest that you appreciate the nature of the difficulty that's holding you up? Are you so absorbed in tackling a difficult item that you spend too long on it and get impatient and annoyed, and feel that your personal pride is being damaged? Not all tests are against time; when they are, there are occasions when it is better to drop an unsatisfactory item than to persist with it.

Be systematic. In aptitude tests which involve practical equipment (assembling mechanisms, for example) take plenty of space, keep together all those things that go together, and don't get in a muddle as you move things around.

Don't be too cautious. Sometimes a candidate tackles an easy item ultra-cautiously, because he thinks it can't be as easy as all that. He suspects a trap.

Be reassured. Nearly all tests are perfectly straight-forward, in the sense that the candidate knows clearly what is expected of him, even if he cannot do it.

Suppose You Don't Land the Job You Want . . .

Do you expect to land the first job you apply for? You will be lucky if you do! It would be like looking in the window of a shop and seeing exactly what you want straight away. It's good advice to 'shop around'.

You, as a younger worker, will shop around for a job that suits you, and employers will 'test the market' (which amounts to the same thing) by seeing a number of applicants and choosing the best.

It's no reflection on you if you aren't picked first time. It might be to your advantage to be turned down, if you have been a bit lazy and not taken the trouble to discover the extent of the market for what you can offer. Being turned down will make you look round. It will also tell you – if you didn't know it already – that it doesn't pay to be too choosy, particularly when jobs are scarce.

If you get as far as an interview for the first job you apply for, and are turned down, at least you will carry away a useful experience. You will know how you were received, and how you perhaps felt a bit inadequate and floored by some of the questions put to you.

Treat it, then, as a warm-up for the next interview – the one that matters. Don't imagine, though, that the second will follow exactly the lines of the first. Employers are individualists, and though the basic questions will be the same, the follow-up questions will probably not be. So don't be disheartened by your 'failure' at the first interview, nor over-confident at the second because you think you have got the measure of the situation.

As a school leaver, you come on to the labour market along with a great many others. At certain times of the year there is a flood of new job hunters. It is a very competitive situation, and it will be a shattering experience for those who put themselves forward with high hopes and expectations, and are turned down at a series of interviews, if indeed their applications reach the interview stage.

There comes a time for many young people, particularly when there is high unemployment, when they must sit down and take stock of the real 'outside world' situation.

First, are you really sure where your strengths lie? If so, it is best to wait until you have exhausted all the local possibilities of employment in your chosen field before you panic.

Take advice from friends, relatives and officials who, between them, know local conditions better than you do. Getting the right kind of job may depend, in the end, on how mobile you are. How far are you prepared to travel, day in, day out, to a job? Are you willing, if necessary, to leave home?

When unemployment is high and there is no job to be found, here are three possibilities you should examine before you take to the dole queue.

First: You might stay on at school for another year (or two years), not just in the hope that 'things will improve' but with a view to improving your education and qualifications. At the same time you may be able to get part-time evening, weekend or holiday jobs to improve your 'track record'.

Second: If you have been turned down for lack of some particular qualification you may be able to fill the gap at Technical College. Get advice from the Careers Office.

Third: School-leavers in the U.K. can apply to go for a year on the Youth Training Scheme, which combines Further Education with practical work experience. Again, Careers Officers can give details.

This may sound like defeatism, but it isn't really. You may, like many others, have left it until rather late in your school career to decide what you really want to do. If so, you may wish you had studied some particular subject more attentively, or to greater depth. Now would be the time to fill any gaps. This course of action may be the best for you, but seek advice first, from those best qualified to give it.

You will naturally talk to others in similar circumstances to yours. You will have to use your own discretion if you are told by a friend (as you might quite well be) that he got fed up with learning and wouldn't go back to school or on to Technical College at any price.

Do you Really Want the Job?

Believe it or not, some candidates who come up for interview don't really want the jobs they have applied for. Some of the others are so half-hearted that they leave it to the interviewer, as a kind of umpire, to make the decision for them. If accepted, they may go ahead with a good heart, and eventually make a success of the job; or they may stick it for a time, and then drift off again.

All this can come about for a variety of reasons. Sometimes, serious doubts arise in a candidate's mind after he has sent off his application. He hasn't resolved them by the time he comes up for interview. He doesn't want to spoil his chances by refusing the job, in case he finally decides to go forward. He leaves his options open – at least for a time.

Some candidates with doubts are the sort who find it hard to make decisions about important things. Basically, they can't face the blame if things go wrong. They are all right in uncomplicated everyday matters, but vital decisions, with consequences that can't be fully known, are a worry and embarrassment to them. They privately heave a sigh of relief whichever way the interviewer's decision goes.

Some candidates can't make up their minds because they don't know who to consult (or whom they can trust). They may fear to disclose their private ideas or ambitions to anyone in case they are frowned on or laughed at. They may feel that the advice given is only what the adviser is paid (or expected) to give, and isn't really tailored to the candidate's individual needs. They may feel that the adviser hasn't the time, or doesn't know enough, to go into the candidate's prospects, with alternatives, in such a way as to carry conviction with the candidate – who is the person who really matters.

On the face of it, a candidate ought to have plenty of advice to go on, with lots of practical knowledge thrown in, from his potential battery of helpers, who may include parents and relations, schoolmasters, friends (including boy- or girl-friends), and official careers and employment officers.

You can add, also, the person-to-person advice that may come from training and personnel officers of firms and officials or organizations whom the candidate may contact, as well as that readily available in books, pamphlets, journals, newspapers and advertisements.

Despite all the help available, some candidates apply for a job, not as the result of a rational decision, but because, for some reason, they have been swept into it by forces they can't control. Many of these candidates are young people who have had the job wished on them, perhaps by parents. They haven't the strength of will to say 'No', and perhaps rely on the interviewer saying 'No' for them.

Some are in this position not because of the machinations of well-meaning parents and friends, or because they lack the will to make a responsible choice for themselves, but because they have left decision-making too late. They need a personal campaign to find and assess the facts well in advance of the critical decision.

Your Second Job

How does an interview for your second job differ from the interview for your first? When you come up for your second job you will be older and more experienced than when you were a raw recruit for your first. You can expect a good deal of questioning on your experience in your first job, your reasons for leaving it, and your reasons for your new application. A good deal may depend on the length of time you were employed in your first job.

If this turned out to be a dead end, no one would be surprised at your wanting to leave. A young worker with enthusiasm and personal resource has every right to leave a job which has no prospects as soon as a better one turns up. But what about a worker in a progressive job which offers chances of promotion to more interesting and responsible work? If he leaves this one without giving it much of a trial, a new employer may suspect that he is a bit work-shy and unwilling to accept responsibility.

It is a good general rule to stay long enough at a job at least to give it a fair trial. If it is a job with prospects, in a good firm, you may decide to stay with it. If you do decide to leave, be clear yourself what your reasons for leaving are. They are bound to be asked when you want to start somewhere else.

Reasons vary a great deal. Marriage and prospects of marriage play an important part for some young people. (E.g. wanting to be near boy- or girl-friend, or near the home young marrieds have set up together.) Gaining wider or different experience is another reason, and so is the wish to join a larger firm, or to start out independently. It is up to the individual whether he really wants to move. To stay too long may label him unambitious, or a dull stick-in-the-mud.

However good his reasons for leaving, he should beware of too many moves in a short period. This may alert a prospective employer to the fact that he might be a drifter, and drift away from him as he has drifted before, so that the employer sees little return from any training he gives him.

Check-List for School-Leavers

1. *Choosing a career*

   Have you considered all the possibilities, and discussed them with parents, teachers and Careers Officers.

   Have you made sure that your choices are possible on the basis of the qualifications you have got or expect to get.

2. *Looking for a job*

   Check newspaper and shop window advertisements every day.

   Keep in constant contact with the Careers Office.

   Call on likely employers even if no job advertised.

   Keep asking friends who are in work whether there are any vacancies.

   Have your referees, exam certificates and testimonials ready all the time.

   Have your c.v. ready.

   Get evening or Saturday jobs to improve your track record.

   Apply for all jobs you like the look of.

3. *Preparing for an interview*

   Be on time or early.

   Dress neatly and put on your best appearance.

   Consider and have a good idea of what wages you expect.

4. *During the interview*

   Be positive – know what you want.

   Be ready with the basic facts about yourself.

   Know why you've applied for that particular job.

   Look, speak and act like the kind of person the employer is looking for.

PART 2

Here, we deal with more sophisticated job-hunting.

How to Prepare Your Application

The careful writing of your application will probably involve the following stages:

1. Make brief jottings on what you expect to include. Gather and check important facts: dates on which you entered and left school; exams passed, with dates and grades; subjects taken; further education; job experience, etc.

    It is worth taking your time over this, perhaps making occasional notes spread over a period of a few days. Otherwise, you may find yourself having to re-cast your application to include fresh material.

    In fact it is well worth keeping a continuous c.v. (see page 18) throughout your working life, and updating it by adding notes every year or so. Otherwise it becomes difficult (say in 20 years time) to remember exactly what you did and when. Obviously you would not regurgitate the whole of this with every job application but pick and choose those elements of it which seem relevant.

2. Make a rough draft. Part of this will be things from the list of facts you have already jotted down, and the other part will be an account of yourself and what you have to offer, etc. You will now be able to judge how it reads, whether it is sensibly organized, and, perhaps, how the reader is likely to take it.

    Although this is called a 'rough draft' a better name might be 'fair copy'. It should be a neat try-out.

There are bound to be a few alterations still to be made, but make sure your rough draft is legible and fit to put in front of someone you can trust for his comments. The important thing is to make all your alterations at this stage, so that there are no deletions, additions, or corrections in the application you actually send. Your rough draft will also give you an idea whether it will fit into the space allotted on the application form. If you really need more space, be bold about it; don't try to cram too much into the space available, but add a fresh sheet.

If you are making several applications around the same time, you can save effort and possibly improve presentation by having a c.v. (not more than one side of typed A4) which can be photocopied and attached to applications.

3. Fill in the application form carefully. This sounds like a blinding glimpse of the obvious, yet in copying from one sheet to another a word or phrase sometimes gets written twice (perhaps because the writer was interrupted at this point), or it may get left out.

If your handwriting is notoriously bad, you must make the effort to write legibly on this important occasion. But don't write such a painstakingly careful hand that all individuality is drained out of it. Some applications are asked for 'in the candidate's own handwriting' (i.e. not typed). If the body to which you are writing believes that handwriting gives a clue to character, you must go along with them in this respect (whatever your private feelings), and see that the clue you provide is positive and acceptable.

Where you are allowed to type, you can type out the draft on plain paper, double-spaced (to leave plenty of room for amendment) then re-check, and think about it for a day or two before typing out the final, which can be single-spaced.

4. Give the application a careful check. It is a curious fact
   that mistakes we make often get overlooked when we
   do the checking ourselves. The simple remedy is to
   persuade someone else to check too.
        Some people work themselves into an agony of
   doubt before sending in an application. You might
   think, before sending in your own application, that
   part of it might be better expressed. Perhaps it might
   be, but unless something positively cries out for
   correction it is better to leave it as it is.

In application forms it is common to ask:
   Surname and forenames; address, telephone number
   Date of birth
   Marital status
   Number and ages of children
   Parent, Guardian, or next-of-kin, with address, tele-
     phone number
   Nationality
   Religion. (This is occasionally asked. Don't be alarmed
     by the question. It may be asked for severely practical
     reasons, e.g. it is well to know when religious obser-
     vances are likely to take the applicant from his work.)
   Questions about health. (Usually very general, but
     specific when it comes to disabilities which might
     affect employment.)
   Details of education and qualifications. (Including
     future plans and exams still to be taken.)
   Details of employment. (Including reasons for leaving
     jobs you have had, and your reasons for leaving your
     present job; including duties and responsibilities in
     your present job, your present pay, and perhaps pay
     in previous jobs; your reasons for making this
     particular application.)
   Details of interests of all kinds
   References
   Questions about: how you learned of the firm you hope
     to join,

relatives employed by the firm,
previous employment in the firm or firms within
the same group,
service in H.M. Forces,
etc.

You may regard a question on 'Pay required . . .' as rather a
sticky one. Bear in mind that the pay you expect should be a
logical continuation of what you have received so far. The
higher the pay you claim, the more searching you can expect
your prospective employer to be in questions of qualifications and relevant experience. You could very well state a
range of pay, so that the employer would understand that the
actual pay is negotiable within that range.

An application form is a confidential document. This is
usually specifically stated (perhaps in the section dealing
with present employment, where it may say that the
employer will not be contacted unless the applicant has been
interviewed. This saves the applicant the embarrassment of
letting his employer know that he is seeking a job elsewhere).

Some forms are neatly-designed all-purpose documents.
They include all the basic facts about the applicant, and all
those things a company or other body needs to know before
accepting him. They include, also, spaces for notes and
assessments made about him at interview, as well as spaces
for checking all the necessary details of accepting him as
employee, student, etc.

Such forms are easily filed, and can be quickly referred to
in case of query or dispute. The candidate will probably not
understand the cryptic (to the outsider) coding of details of
receiving him into the firm or organization, but he does have
a chance of seeing how much space is allotted to interview
notes and assessments, and can therefore to some extent
gauge its importance.

The all-purpose nature of such forms sometimes makes
the applicant wonder why on earth they want to know all the
information they seek. In one part of the form, he fills in the
line which asks him what kind of appointment he is looking

for, and in another he is asked whether he speaks a foreign language (and if so, how well), and whether he holds a driving licence. Perhaps his preferred employment demands neither.

It is just as well to complete the form fully. Jobs change, and new opportunities come up and are offered to those in a position to grasp them. If you have applied for a particular job which turns out not to be open to you, your application may stay in the files until a similar one comes along. If your application was a general one, asking for appointment whenever a suitable vacancy occurs, the more information you can give the better. This advice is reinforced by the fact that forms sometimes ask what other work you are able to do. (Don't say 'Any'. This is too vague. It couldn't be true, anyhow. Be as specific as you can.)

Some application forms are rounded off in the simplest possible way with the date and signature of the applicant. The applicant has given his information, and the signature testifies to its correctness.

Sometimes this is put formally: 'I hereby certify that the answers given are true to the best of my belief' (or words to that effect). Occasionally, this is extended to include a declaration that the applicant has not withheld any information which might be to his disadvantage.

Young people applying for an apprenticeship within an industry or trade may need to make a formal application counter-signed by parent or guardian.

References and Testimonials

References are different from testimonials but people sometimes confuse them.

A *reference* is confidential. When you leave a job it is sensible (if you have done well there) to ask your erstwhile employer if you can give his name as a reference – and this means that new employers to whom you apply may contact the referee to find out things about you.

A *testimonial* is of less value. It is often a typewritten sheet of paper given by the employer to someone who is leaving – which can then be shown to other potential employers.

References

You probably have to give the names of one or two referees with your application. Who do you ask to act for you?

It must be someone who knows you well enough to be able to give reliable help to whomever deals with your application. It must also be someone of good standing who can give an unprejudiced appraisal of you.

It is no use having as referee a friend who will stick up for you come what may, so that his praise may be suspect, particularly if the reader of his reference has cause to wonder whether some damaging facts have been omitted or glossed over. If the reader does not find the information he expects in a reference, he may 'read between the lines' and suspect that it is not there because it would not support your case.

A reference with too many superlatives is unlikely to be balanced enough to be really helpful; if it is too critical, it might spoil your chances. The best kind of reference is one which the reader feels to be frank and balanced, so that any criticisms are offset by positive recommendations which carry conviction.

The reader will want to know how long your referee has

known you – and how recently. His reference wouldn't be much use if he knew you ten years ago but has since lost touch with you.

This raises a practical matter for you. Never use a person's name as a referee without his permission. If you put in several applications shortly after getting his agreement, there is no reason why you should not use his name for all of them. But if some time elapses between one round of applications and the next, it is as well to express your thanks and ask him to renew his permission.

It is a small thing for you to give a person's name and address on your application and then sit back and await developments. To a referee it can be a bit of a chore if he is asked for a reference at a particularly busy time.

He won't want to handicap you by failing to answer, or by delaying his answer so that it doesn't arrive in time. If he is interested enough in you to back your application, you can at least tell him the eventual outcome. (Be cautious about ringing him up to discover whether he has been asked for a reference. Understandably, you are on tenterhooks wondering whether you will be called to interview. But unless you know your referee *very* well, he may feel that these demands on his attention are getting too much, and begin to regret that he ever undertook the task at all.)

It is quite possible that the person who considers your application will not only ask for a reference, but follow-up with a telephone call to your referee to fill in any gaps or answer a few queries. This may be necessary so that the interviewer is as fully informed as possible by the time he meets you.

Testimonials

For the same reason, your interviewer may ring up the writer of a testimonial. (Never send an original, *always* a copy.)

Testimonials have two disadvantages from the point of view of an interviewer: they date, and they are seen by the applicant. The interviewer may wonder whether anything

has happened since a testimonial was written to cause the
writer to change his mind about you, or whether there are
fresh facts that he would add if he were writing it now. (You
can help yourself here by asking the writer of an old
testimonial to re-date it, or revise it, before you send a copy
with your application. Testimonials over five years old are
probably of doubtful value. In the course of time, as you
gather fresh experience, they are superseded by more up-to-
date ones.)

References are confidential, and therefore more candid
than testimonials. The writers of both are probably just as
honest as one another, but the writers of testimonials are
likely to spare themselves embarrassment about referring to
one's limitations by tactful omissions.

Testimonials are rather general, and can be used in
whatever way the applicant thinks fit. References, on the
other hand, are specific. The referee is given details of the
particular appointment or place that the applicant is
seeking, so he knows the context in which his reference will
be used. There is an advantage to an applicant here, because
the referee can emphasize qualities and skills that are
appropriate in this context.

The Course of the Interview

All interviews differ in style and approach. The following suggestions are by no means exhaustive but provide a framework which *might* be experienced.

Some things for you to bear in mind

Some things your interviewer is thinking about

1. The courtesies

It helps you to know your interviewer by name. He is a person too! If he is the right man for this kind of job, his warmth of manner will put you at ease from the start.

He already knows your name, and he won't want to put you to the disadvantage of addressing him as 'Mr Er – er', or compel you to call him 'Sir', which sometimes sounds unnecessarily subservient.

Don't sit down until you have been offered a chair, but, equally, don't stand shifting from foot to foot as if you wanted to visit the toilet.

When you sit, if there is a slight delay while the interviewer adjusts his papers, don't fidget or look round the room. Sit alertly and

I need to break the ice quickly. Is the candidate mature and reasonably confident, or does he need helping? (Perhaps by extra sympathy of manner, or by sharing a humorous aside with him. There is nothing like a light touch of humour for getting over a sticky patch, either now or later on.)

What is my first impression of him? If it is favourable, I must probe the substance behind the initial charm.

If it is unfavourable, it is up to me to draw him out. It would be a pity to miss a sound candidate because for some innocent reason he does not interview well.

Some things for you to bear in mind	Some things your interviewer is thinking about

wait until he is ready. (This applies also if there is an interruption – for example, a telephone call – while the interview is taking place.)

2. Checking the facts

Don't assume that, because the interviewer is going over the main facts of your application, he has not already read it with attention. He needs to check the facts to make sure he has fully understood them, to fill any gaps, and to add details to any information that seems a bit scanty.

This is your chance to get used to the sound of the interviewer's voice and his way of putting things.

He is setting a standard in the businesslike conduct of the interview, and you should respond accordingly.

Be ready to offer any supplementary information that you think may help. Don't give it in great detail, but don't withhold it if it helps to round off the picture he is getting of you.

Along with the facts go the reasons: (e.g. 'Why did

I have already made some private notes on points I wish to pursue with the candidate. I will check with him particularly those facts I want to follow up later.

Often an 'all-comers' application form does not ask all the questions relevant to specific interviewees. I must ask any such questions now, in a relaxed, face-to-face situation, rather than seek answers later by correspondence.

Some things for you to bear in mind

Some things your interviewer is thinking about

you leave your last job?' 'Why did you study these subjects at a school when another group of subjects might have given you a better chance?', etc.) Give them briefly and frankly.

3. Following up

The interviewer may raise some points from the confidential papers he has about you, or from telephone inquiries he has made.

This is the stage where the interviewer will begin to talk less and expect you to talk more. (E.g. inviting you to describe and develop some experience you have referred to: 'Tell me about . . .' 'What happened when . . .')

This is the time to go over any apparent discrepancies there may be between what the candidate wrote in his application and any other information I have about him. Often such discrepancies are easily explained; where they are not, the reasons may come out later in the interview.

Now to get the candidate talking. My attention is no longer divided between the sheaf of documents and the candidate. I can now give him my full attention, with only an occasional glance at my notes.

If my notes occupy too much of my attention it will prove that I haven't done my homework properly.

4. Basic questions

Now we are getting more

Up to now, the interview

Some things for you to bear in mind	Some things your interviewer is thinking about

to the point. He is sizing me up. He knows my qualifications and experience; now he is asking himself whether I am the right kind of person for the place, and whether I am easy to get on with.

He won't learn this from brief, one-word answers. I must expand a bit, without throwing my weight about or being garrulous.

The interview is moving along quite well and I think I am making the right kind of impression.

If I can do well under stress – and you can't say that there's no stress about an interview – he'll know that I can cope with quite a bit.

has centred on the candidate's application and the supporting material. Now the emphasis must shift to the position he hopes to fill.

I know the kind of person we are looking for, and I am learning quite a lot about the candidate. Soon I shall have to make up my mind whether I can see him successfully coping with what the position demands.

I shall have to tell him all those things that can't really be expressed in an advertisement, but are better told in a relaxed person-to-person way at the actual interview.

I shall be interested in his reaction because it will reveal whether he can see *himself* successfully occupying the position.

If the candidate has any doubts about whether he really wants what he has put in for, now is the time to find out.

5. Further questions in depth

He's going into more detail now. He wouldn't do this if he wasn't interested in me.

If the candidate himself has expressed some doubt about whether he really wants to proceed with his

Some things for you to bear in mind

Now is my chance to show my strength. I think it pays, though, to be frank about any failures or disappointments that may come up. I can balance these by expanding on things that have gone well and my hopes for the future. Perhaps he'll let me lead off from some of his questions to other things that might help me but that he doesn't yet know about.

Some things your interviewer is thinking about

application, he need not detain me much longer. Nor need I keep a candidate who has already shown that he is definitely not the kind of person we are looking for.

But the majority of interviewees, who show acceptable qualities, are worth probing further, to see what extra strengths they have to offer. The 'plus' qualities will probably be decisive – unless the field is a very poor one.

Our conversation has already suggested some possibilities worth pursuing now.

I must also find out about anything which might prevent the candidate giving of his best. (Family tensions? Absorbing outside interests that could be a source of strength, but carried too far may mean weakness?) I have to be tactful here, because I must not go beyond our legitimate concern.

6. An opportunity for the candidate to present further facts or to ask questions

This really is the last chance. If I have nothing else to say, at least I can round

My questioning has set trains of thought going in his mind as well as mine. This is

Some things for you to bear in mind

Some things your interviewer is thinking about

off the interview with a comment which compliments the interviewer on covering the ground so thoroughly by his questions that I am satisfied now to leave it to him.

his last chance to round off the picture of himself.

I can also settle any doubts in answering his questions.

I shall perhaps be able to gauge his interest and enthusiasm by the sort of questions he asks.

7. Rounding it off

I now know how long my period of suspense will be, but I wonder whether I can tell from his manner whether I have been successful?

Anyway, I will leave confidently and on good terms with him. Even if I am unsuccessful this has been a useful and interesting experience.

I must tell him when he can expect to learn the result of the interview.

I may be able to give him an indication of success; but whether I can or not, I can at least express an interest in him and in what he had to offer. I hope he leaves feeling that he has had a fair hearing.

Don't Let Anything Throw You Off Balance!

It is easy to give advice like this, but, humanly speaking, no one can guarantee himself a cool and relaxed interview in all circumstances. The best we can do is to be aware of things that might put us to disadvantage and perhaps sap our confidence.

An interviewer needs to probe beneath our guard, to discover a real person, with strengths and weaknesses. Strengths are respected and their potentialities assessed; the extent of weaknesses needs to be known, and so does our capacity to remedy them. (Education and training will put right some weaknesses.)

Some weaknesses are personal to ourselves. If you have a tendency to blush, stammer, or show obvious signs of nervousness, you may be sure that a 'stress' situation like an interview is more likely to bring it on than a casual chat about nothing in particular. If you are apt to resent 'prying' into your affairs, you may not like some of the personal questions that are bound to be asked, and your emotional temperature will rise accordingly. If this happens, you will not find it easy to gather or express your thoughts, and you will probably become very self-conscious about the impression you are creating. In an emotionally charged situation like this, you could quite easily misread your interviewer's attitude and intentions towards you. He probably feels more sympathetic than you think.

It doesn't do to be too sensitive. Take the situation as philosophically as you can. Look outward rather than inward. Concentrate on the interviewer as well as his questions. Try him with a smile. Keep your attention on his face (but not so fixedly that you look as if you'd like to murder him). You are the focus of his attention: let him be the focus of yours.

Like most people, you are probably not unduly sensitive, and you can answer up for yourself in a reasonably forthright yet courteous manner. What, then, can go wrong?

Here are some things that may affect you:

1. *The pace of questions may hot up.*

    The interviewer may be aware of other candidates whom he must see. The programme of interviews may be running late, and he doesn't want delays to get worse.

    Or, he may find the interview with you dragging a bit, and force the pace in a way which is a cue to you to get a move on.

    Or, he may think you have a tendency to ramble or introduce irrelevancies, so he fires brief questions at you to keep you to the point. (*His* point, remember.)

    Or he may want to see how you cope with questions that crowd in on each other. Do you easily get rattled? Can you deal with them at a fast pace? (Being able to respond quickly and adequately to matters that arise suddenly might be vital in the job you are seeking.) If you are rather deliberate in your thought and speech, don't let your interviewer hurry you unduly. He may respect you more for the seriousness with which you take his questions than for the rather trivial, staccato, off-the-cuff answers you may be tempted to give.

2. *Questions may switch suddenly from one topic to another.*

    This can happen because the main themes of the interview have been covered, and the interviewer wants to settle a number of points to round off his picture of you.

    A sudden change of topic catches nearly everyone off guard, so an interviewer may use this method if he suspects that there are matters you wish to avoid, or to cover up.

    He may use the method, too, to return to a topic on

which he was not really satisfied with your earlier answers.

3. *Your interviewer may make remarks which have an 'edge' to them, and which you may find unfair, so that, in self-defence, you feel compelled to reply to set the record straight.*

He might say, for example, 'I am getting the impression that you're willing to do things that you're interested in, but resent being asked to do others, however vital they are'.

Or, bluntly, 'I think you're lazy'.

Perhaps he means to shake you out of complacency with needling remarks, or perhaps he is voicing aloud doubts that he has at the back of his mind.

If this happens to you, try not to feel aggressive, or too much on the defensive. Take the criticism seriously. It is better to know how you appear to an interviewer than to be left in the dark and perhaps give a similarly unfortunate impression at the next interview.

You might begin by saying 'I think I know why I have given you this impression, but . . .' If you can go some way towards agreeing with a criticism before you offer a more favourable explanation, at least you will show that you can recognize a fault in yourself, and perhaps that you are doing something to correct it.

If you refuse to accept a well-meant criticism, your interviewer may think as badly of you for believing 'He's got it all wrong' as you think of him. You don't make a friend of your interviewer in this way.

Any Matters Arising?

When the details on your written application have been checked, they are almost certain to suggest further questions to your interviewer. The actual questions will depend on the nature of your application, but you will have no difficulty in judging which of the following lines of inquiry could arise in your particular case. The questions below will probably not be asked as they are given, but they are indications of what is in the interviewer's mind:

Your education

Was your education what might have been expected for one of your ability and background?

Did anything hold you back, or, on the other hand, give you any advantages?

Did you make steady progress during your school (College, University) career?

Did you rise to the opportunities offered by your school (College, University) to gain qualifications?

How do you account for any exam failures you have had, particularly in vital subjects? How do you account for any persistent failure in a subject important to you?

Do you expect success in any exams coming up?

Have you got the right balance of subjects for a person of your particular talents?

Are your subjects so broadly based that they don't really reveal your strengths? Or are they so narrowly specialist that they aren't much use to you unless an employer wants exactly what you offer and no more?

Are there any unexpected gaps in the subjects (or qualifications) you have to offer? If so, what are you doing to remedy them?

At what level are your passes? Couldn't you have done better?

Why didn't you take this subject? Why did you drop that? Why didn't you carry the other to a higher level?

Your work

Changes of job. Why? Why so many (so few) changes? Did all the changes lead to greater experience, more responsibility, promotion?

How long did you stay in your last job? (Or, why do you want to leave your present job?)

Do you enjoy your work? Job-satisfaction: what does this mean to you? What really motivates you?

What do you expect to get from the job for which you are applying that you don't get from your present job? What have you really got to offer us?

Do you understand what the job for which you are applying entails?

How did you hear of us?

What was the exact nature of the work in your last (present) job?

What degree of responsibility did you hold?

Bear in mind that questions arise from testimonials and references as well as from your written application. This is especially true of the most recent stages of your career, whether in some form of education or at work.

You know what your testimonials say, because you sent in copies with your application yourself, and you must have a fair idea of what your referees have said about you. Now put yourself in the position of your interviewer: could any questions arise from the information or views they have expressed about you?

Some Questions You Should Be Prepared For

When you come up for interview you probably have a fair idea of what you are likely to be asked. You may be surprised, though, at the range of questions fired at you, and you may feel that some of them pry unnecessarily into your private affairs.

How can it be anyone else's concern, you may wonder, how you spend your free time? If you are married, you may feel suspicious if you are asked whether your wife (or husband) supports you in your application. Surely this is your own business, and no one else's.

Now look at it in this way. Would you feel happy if the people for whom you worked regarded you merely as a pair of hands? Or as an able-bodied robot? Or as a set of skills to be used according to demand? You would more likely want to shriek out that you are a person too, with human wants and feelings and rights.

The wider questions asked at interview help to fill out the picture of you as a person. They help to show whether you are likely to 'fit in', whether you are easy to get on with, whether you possess ambition and are likely to work hard, or be a frequent absentee. They help to show whether you possess the requisite qualities and have the time, the energy, and the will to use them.

Those making appointments are only too well aware of the family, social, and economic pressures that can turn an otherwise satisfactory person into a harassed individual doing slapdash work and exercising a demoralizing influence on others. A good background is therefore reassuring to those making appointments. Can you blame them for not wanting to buy trouble?

In cases like these, frankness is important. There should be no hint of holding back, or concealing what might be a bit damaging.

You might agree about the importance of frankness, but what is the good of frankness if it leads to your application being turned down without an interview at all?

There is a possible compromise here. You might faithfully fill in your application form without drawing attention to an awkward fact, and rely on giving the proper background and interpretation to it in the person-to-person interview situation. In this situation you will at least get a hearing, and almost certainly the chance to establish your sincerity by your speech and bearing. If there is anything to your detriment, it is best to say it yourself and get it over with, rather than have it dragged from you. Say it, and move quickly on to more favourable ground.

Sometimes you have simply got to refer to an awkward fact at the application stage. An example of this is when you lack what is usually regarded as an essential qualification.

If you made no reference to the omission, they might simply think that you hadn't properly read the conditions, and put your application straight into the waste paper basket. In the space where you were expected to enter details of the qualification you could put 'Please see covering letter', or 'Please see general remarks at end'.

The covering letter solution is probably better than trying to fit an explanation into the small space they allow on most forms. See that the letter is firmly clipped or fastened to the form, and don't let yourself be lured into such a lengthy explanation that the letter is unlikely to be read.

A problem for the interviewer is how far he can take the candidate's word on questions about himself. Can he believe him all along the line? Is the candidate a yes-man (for the purpose of the interview) anxious to please and to be well-thought-of? Will his determination to gain acceptance outweigh his honesty?

One way of checking is for the interviewer to ask a good many questions and to see whether a consistent pattern emerges. If it doesn't, the candidate may be confronted at a later stage with a statement he made earlier and asked to explain the difference.

Spontaneous, straightforward answers given without hesitation carry conviction, particularly if they are backed up by a frank, open manner.

When an interviewer suspects that a candidate is 'going along' with him, agreeing a shade too readily with his line of thought and not expressing any doubts or qualifications, he may test the candidate with some statement bordering on the outrageous, and then express surprise that the candidate agreed with it.

This can happen so innocently. Beware of being lured gently on, perhaps with a line of thought you hadn't previously considered. You say 'Yes' almost mechanically, and are then faced with the logic of the position you have taken up.

You need to be cautious (but not irritatingly ultra-cautious) and to think before you answer. If you don't understand a question, ask the interviewer to repeat it, or to put it in a different way. Or you can re-phrase it yourself, asking 'Do you mean . . .?'

Another approach is to think your answer out aloud, prefacing what you say with the comment that the question has several implications, and going on to give what you think is involved, before attempting a final answer.

No interviewer expects a candidate to be a human slot-machine from which pops an immediate complete answer. If you give a quick response to every question asked, you could be suspected of saying the first thing that comes into your head and sticking to it, right or wrong. Don't be afraid to admit that an answer was a bit hasty, and that on further thought you would put it differently.

Among the subjects which can lead to follow-up questions which might betray you into giving ill-considered judgements are the following:

> Explanations of why your education or career took the line it did.
>
> Criticisms of teachers, employers, authorities.
>
> Opinions you express on people, firms, policies.
>
> Likes and dislikes. Personal preferences.

'I see you had an interview for . . . You weren't accepted. What went wrong?'

Bear in mind that a question is not always what it seems to be. For example, the interviewer might ask a candidate 'Do you ever lose your temper? (or get excited, shout at anyone, enjoy an argument)' but the question at the back of his mind may be rather different. It could be 'Are you as dull as you seem to be?'

Or, it might be 'You sound a bit opinionated. Are you aggressive with it? Do you rub people up the wrong way?'

Or might it simply be a wish to see another side of the candidate. If he has been fairly forthcoming, yet too smoothly neutral, his interviewer may hope to see the light of enthusiasm (or battle, or protest) in his eyes.

Qustion and answer are stimulus and response. The right question will provoke an informative answer – and not just in the form of words.

The words have got to be right, of course, but in giving them the candidate reveals much more. He shows:

> how quickly he appreciates the point of what he is being asked,
> how he marshals the facts before he replies,
> how he handles an account, an argument, an explanation,
> what his priorities are, and what he selects for emphasis,
> what he rejects, or dismisses as insignificant,
> in gesture (sometimes in place of words, and sometimes in support of them) he may show surprise, annoyance, perplexity, anxiety, fear, hope, enlightenment, etc.

Some candidates use the vocabulary of gesture much more than others. This is particularly so with face and hands but also with shifts of position and direction of glance.

Words can be used to conceal as well as reveal. It is less easy to conceal through gesture. If a candidate made up his mind to prevent his gestures from revealing his private hopes or anxieties he would probably sit stiff and poker-faced, and create the same impression as if he answered every question with a monosyllable or brief phrase. If the interviewer could not draw him out he might be dismissed as one with little to offer.

It is part of an interviewer's job to see that a candidate does not lose by showing a nervousness which is perfectly natural and understandable.

The easiest and most relaxing question you might be asked at interview is the simple one 'You're nervous, aren't you?' and with a nod, a smile, and a deep breath your nervousness has gone.

'What do you read?'

This is one of a number of questions designed to discover a candidate's alertness, his common observation, and his interest in people, things, and ideas.

Variations on this question are:

'Do you read for information?'

Most practical people do. They needn't feel ashamed of missing the classics of literature. Their temperament and talent lead them to facts, know-how, and personal skills. The interviewer will be interested to learn whether their factual reading is up-to-date and links adequately with their aims; whether it is understood and critically received. The practical person can surely be expected to be aware of the magazines, journals, and newspaper columns which cater for his interests. More than this: he can be expected to be taking a close and continuing interest in them.

'Do you read for pleasure?'

This seems a lightweight question, but answers to it sometimes throw considerable light on whether or not the candidate is a well-balanced individual. Is he such a serious-minded specialist that he is blind to the influences that affect other people? If so, how is he going to get on with them in his work? Is he already in a mental rut that he will find it harder and harder to get out of?

You, as a candidate, needn't fear earning a low opinion because you read Agatha Christie (or whoever else you care to name) rather than Shakespeare. If your reading gives you pleasure, at least the question touches your enthusiasm, and you can be expected to say why you enjoy your favourite author or why you like a certain type of book.

It is a painful experience for an interviewer to see a candidate who reads very little, or nothing at all, dredging up from his memory the title of a book read long ago. If you can't do better than say 'Black Beauty' (an answer I have heard to this question) it is best to shut up.

'What newspaper do you read?'

It doesn't matter what newspaper you name. It is the follow-up that concerns your interviewer. What do you look for in the paper, and what do you think you get out of it?

This is a question which sometimes leads to a good deal of verbal sparring without much information. The interviewer wants to know what catches your eye and makes you read further. He wants to know what you positively seek out in the paper. He might ask what you read first, and then next.

It's no use claiming to read 'everything'. Your interviewer will raise his eyebrows and probably repeat the word. 'Everything?' And then you will have to climb down and say what you do read.

It's not very informative, either, to claim that you read the headlines. You probably do. He is more interested in the kind of headline that encourages you to read on.

In getting you to talk about the newspaper, your interviewer won't want to feel that he's putting ideas into your head. If you are vague about your reading, he won't want to have to ask you whether you prefer home news to foreign, or sport to both of them. He won't want to name the various sections of the paper so that you can say 'Yes' to the one that sounds most promising. He'll end by suspecting, perhaps rightly, that you don't read the papers at all, except to see the headlines you couldn't possibly miss, the sports results you are interested in, and the big advertisement spreads.

A wider form of question is: *'From what source do you get most of your knowledge of the world around you?'*

It might be from the newspaper, from TV, from radio, or from discussions with your friends.

You should be prepared to follow up a question like this in whatever direction your interviewer takes it:

Writers, programmes, personalities you have come to rely on (or admire, or despise, etc.). What is there about them that inspires your interest (admiration, contempt, etc.)?

Are you a random viewer (listener, reader), switching off if a programme is not to your liking, or do you positively look out for particular programmes (people, topics)?

Do you discuss world (local, political) affairs with your friends?

Be prepared for a ruthlessly factual question or two:
'What's in the papers today?'
'What important event is taking place in ...?'
'What is your opinion on the controversy about ...?

'How do you use your spare time?'
A wide range of interests suggests a lively mind and an active person. It also suggests a body of experience and personal resource that can be drawn on.

It might, though, point to a nervously active person who attempts a lot of things and drops them at the first sign of difficulty.

Your interviewer will probably try to find out how long and successfully your interests have been pursued, and whether you still keep them up. It's not a good thing to claim, as a piece of window-dressing, that you are interested in a hobby or sport, and then have your interviewer discover that in fact you dropped it years ago. It doesn't matter dropping a

pursuit: your interviewer understands as well as you do the
pressures on an individual in a busy world.

Questioning you about your spare time will soon tell an
interviewer whether you are easily bored or whether you live
a full and satisfying life. 'There's nothing to do' tells more
about the speaker than about his opportunities. Bored
people who live empty lives are more likely to be unhappy
and a source of unhappiness in others than people who live
busy and varied lives. An interviewer is bound to be
concerned with the effect of a candidate he accepts on those
with whom he mixes.

There is another thing your interviewer will be concerned
with. Is your life so full, and are you subject to such pressure,
that you won't be able to cope with the work properly if he
accepts you? (If you fear giving this impression, you could
say what you would drop if you find you've taken on too
much.)

Questions concerning spare time can cover such wide
ground that they can quite easily touch sensitive spots.
Suppose you are an active political worker, or a keen
supporter of a particular church, or have family (or boy-
friend or girl-friend) troubles – are you expected to be
forthcoming about these too? Would it pay (or tell against
you) to identify yourself with a political party, or a church
that might not have your interviewer's approval?

Discussion is more free and open these days than it used to
be, and it is easy to exaggerate the fear that your private
beliefs will be frowned on. (Come to that, your interviewer
might share them.)

In sensitive areas it is best to proceed with caution but not
concealment. You can mention political activities or church
activities or family matters and leave it to your interviewer to
pursue things further if he wants to. After all, it is better to
show an active concern for political or religious or social
affairs than to appear to be the kind of person who leaves all
these important things to others.

On a severely practical level, don't become aggressive or
defensive or long-winded about sensitive subjects that come
up. Let them simply take their limited place in the interview.

'Do you have any cultural interests?'
'Culture' means different things to different people. In an interview context you can take it to mean, simply, 'way of life'. Questions on cultural interests have little or no direct connection with the purpose of your application, or with your interviewer's eventual acceptance or rejection of you.

They are justified because your interviewer is looking at you as a whole person, and not as a pair of hands, a set of skills, or a body of knowledge. Your person-to-person relationships are likely to be all the better if you have wide cultural interests.

(The importance of wide interests is well recognised nowadays. It is the reason, for example, for including liberal studies – under this or some other name – in College courses, and for the provision of sports and recreational facilities for workpeople.)

An interviewer may spend much time in questioning you about sport, going to the theatre or cinema, or about TV programmes, but you should not regard it as an intrusion if he does ask a few questions. The same applies to questions on travel here or abroad, holidays you have had, visits you have made, bodies you belong to, people you have met, classes you have attended, and all the miscellaneous things that have interested you.

He is likely to react more favourably where you are an active participant rather than a casual, fairly passive, observer.

'What are your ambitions?'
Or, 'What's your long-term view of this application of yours?'

Have you just applied hopefully, so that if you are accepted you will heave a sigh of relief, flop down in a chair, and say 'I'm there!' Or have you taken a long view of your career, and see your present application as a stage in the planned development and use of your abilities?

It makes a difference! You may be successful with a hopeful and lucky application, but you may drift off again with a similar application elsewhere. But the more you have thought about your career, and planned it in general terms as well as you are able, the more you are likely to gain (and to give) if your application is successful. Your work and progress will be purposive, and you will not be so likely to give up at the first difficulty.

From the interviewer's point of view, it is important that the work should be at your level. He will want to make up his mind whether you are such an able person that you are likely to be dissatisfied with the work, and therefore want to move off at the earliest opportunity (or become a thorn in the flesh). Or whether you will perhaps not be up to the work, and get fed up with it and your lack of progress, with unfortunate consequences for all concerned.

How long you are likely to stay is a critical question. If you're not going to stay long, is it worth saying 'Yes' to your application when they will shortly be looking for someone else to replace you?

Your interviewer needs to be sure that you know what work would be involved if he accepted you. He can bring this out through his questions. To reinforce the answers you give him he may also ask 'How did you get to know of us?' 'Who have you talked to about your application?' 'Where did you get advice from?' 'Have you studied the information we sent with the application form?'

He may even ask 'What do you know about our work?'

You will be able to deduce some questions he will actually ask you from the questions he is bound to ask himself about you:

Has he set his sights too high (too low)?

Will he be a round peg in a square hole?

Is he really committed to us (our work, etc.) or is his application a second-choice one because he couldn't get his first choice? If it is a second-choice (because his first choice was not available, or because he applied for it and was turned down) has he become reconciled to it? Has he really thought about what his choice involves?

Is he cut out for some of the things we do, but not for others? If so, does he expect us to keep him at the things he knows and likes best, so that he can avoid the rest? Doesn't he realise that he must take the rough with the smooth, and accept some unwelcome duties with a good heart?

Ambitions are revealing because they show some degree of self-assessment.

Some ambitions form part of an individual's fantasy-world, and are hopelessly unrealistic. Applications based on fantasy are a try-on. Most people have a sufficiently realistic assessment of their own abilities and interests not to waste their own and others' time on fruitless applications, but some are so blinkered that they don't realise their limitations.

'After all, if you don't bung in an application, you'll never know your luck, will you?' is the attitude they take. Most unrealistic applications are sifted out at the application stage; very few lead to a call-up for interview. But all interviewers face, at one time or another, the odd candidate who causes the interviewer to wonder, in the course of the conversation, how on earth he came to be called up at all. An interview like this is likely to be brief, polite, and conclusive.

(An interviewer is probably used to telling candidates that they will be told the result of the interview by letter in a week or so, and he may adopt this method with the odd unsatisfactory candidate under discussion. He could express his regret and explain why the application must fail, but he is more likely to spare himself a wrangle by sticking to the usual formula. This is a pity in one way, because the candidate may put in an equally hopeless application elsewhere, and feel that, when he fails again, he didn't stand a chance. If he lowered his sights he wouldn't lay himself so wide open to disappointment.)

Don't be afraid to reveal your hopes and ambitions. Your own thought about them beforehand rules out all but the tiniest possibility that they contain an element of fantasy. Expressing reasonable (and even rather hopeful) ambitions may well reinforce the view your interviewer already holds of you as a person with something about him. After all, ambition argues a willingness to work hard in order to achieve it.

'What do you think you have to offer us?'
This is a difficult question, however it is phrased. It might be expressed, a little more delicately, in this way: 'What qualities, do you think, are needed by . . . (the position you are applying for)?'

You answer this, of course, in a considered and detached way, but as your list lengthens you begin to suspect that you already know the follow-up question. You are probably right. It is: 'Do you think you possess these qualities?'

Putting the question in two parts, like this, is a good deal kinder and less embarrassing than asking it in its bluntest form. But even the blunt question can be put more devastatingly: 'What makes you think that you would make a good . . .?'

Whichever way it comes, be prepared for a fairly downright question on your own assessment of what you have to give – and what it takes. Your interviewer may ease it for you by inviting you not to be too modest.

The question repays careful preparation. You would be lucky if you could draw out of thin air an answer which would withstand a probing follow-up. Yet you don't want to reel off an answer so pat that you have obviously learnt it up.

Self-assessment by a candidate is very revealing from the interviewer's point of view. The candidate is really doing two things. He is selecting the qualities he believes are called for and, by implication, putting them into an order of importance. He is also setting out the qualities he believes he possesses and matching them with the first list. He is both auctioneer and bidder.

Whether the question takes you by surprise, or whether you have thought about it beforehand, don't be afraid to take your time. If you blurt out the first thing that comes into your head you will only be written down as a person who speaks before he thinks.

Pay your interviewer the compliment of taking a difficult

question seriously. He will be watching your reaction very closely.

Such a question ought not to take you by surprise. After all, you did put in an application. You must have considered your prospects and your chances.

You can get your ideas moving with a very brief reiteration of the qualifications, personal skills and experience you set down in your written application. You might then refer to the following matters, in whatever order you think best;

Getting on with people (a *must* in every job)
Acceptance of responsibility
Ability to give and take orders
Understanding what the firm (undertaking, public body, College, to which you have applied) stands for
Interests or ideas you would like to pursue if accepted
Personal qualities: loyalty, co-operativeness, initiative, etc.

Take your time – but try not to ramble on. Leave it to your interviewer to ask you to enlarge on any matter, or to bring your answer to a conclusion. He will stop you when he has heard enough.

Hypothetical questions

The interviewer may create an imaginary (or real) situation and ask you how you would deal with it – the 'what if . . .' question.

Reply to these questions with care. The situation described may be very similar to a real one which happened recently, and a detailed answer from you may be wrong because you only have a brief description of the position. Answer by explaining the general principles you would apply to such a problem, and perhaps say what you have done in the past in similar circumstances.

Women having babies

A young married woman with no children is likely to be

asked about her plans for a family. This may be an important factor if there is training or re-training involved, and in any case the legal provisions on maternity leave can cause problems, especially for smaller employers.

If you have definitely planned to delay starting a family, then say so, and for how long. Otherwise you will have to be vague, but don't raise the subject unless the question is asked.

Have I the Personality for the Job?

One basic question that your interviewer will have to make up his mind about is 'Has he the right personality for the job?'

He will have a preliminary answer or two before he ever sees you. These will come from testimonials and references, from any follow-up telephone calls he might make, and to a limited extent from your own application. He must fill in the rest of the picture from his meeting with you.

Sometimes it is not so much a question of filling in gaps at interview as of revising what he thought he knew about you.

The picture one forms from a written description, no matter how honestly done, is often very different from the reality. An interviewer may, on very rare occasions, have to look through his papers to make sure that they are indeed about the candidate in front of him.

The picture that emerges from interview is developed along the lines of what the interviewer wishes to learn. It can be as detailed and accurate as his skill allows. But the picture from the documents depends on what the writers wished to tell. It may be as helpful or misleading as an Identikit picture. It fails, as all verbal descriptions do, when words mean different things to different people. It fails, sometimes, because the writer of the description does not always have the intimate, up-to-date knowledge of the candidate that the interviewer assumes he has. (A question on the reference form may help to settle this. 'How well do you know the candidate?' 'Very well/fairly well/slightly' gives useful information, especially when coupled with the question 'How long have you known the candidate?')

It may fail, on a small but unknown number of occasions, because a reference is not quite the honest description it purports to be.

The interviewer himself must not fail. The crucial 'Yes' or 'No' depends on his assessment.

He must therefore use some tried and reliable method of assessing all those qualities which can be lumped together under the heading of Personality.

Hunches won't do. The candidate would be at a gross disadvantage if his interviewer thought 'I wouldn't trust him round the corner' as soon as he clapped eyes on him. Or an unfair advantage if the interviewer was beguiled by blue eyes, a ready smile, and an open countenance into thinking that he was just the man for the job.

It wouldn't do, either, if he thought that a candidate couldn't possibly be any good if his eyes were too close together, or if he had a 'lean and hungry look'.

You can't pick interview winners any more than you can pick criminal types on simple rules of thumb like these.

Written personality tests are nowhere near as useful in practice as one might think they should be. At best, they can supplement an interview, and alert an interviewer to a candidate's potential in certain areas – exceptional promise, for example, or weakness likely to lead to failure.

Yet we can take our cue from what such tests attempt. Basically, a personality test is a test of attitudes. If you knew the attitude a person adopts on a sufficiently wide and representative range of issues, you would know all you would need to know about his personality.

The interviewer tries to find out how the candidate looks at life, particularly in those areas that have some bearing on the job for which a decision about him must be made.

Your interviewer already knows what your qualifications are. He knows the levels of your achievement, and (assuming that you did yourself justice on your application form) what further qualifications you hope for. He should also know (making the same assumption) of your membership of any bodies, particularly professional, semi-professional, or 'learned', whose membership implies an important degree of recognition.

Now he wants to look at the person behind the

qualifications: the real *you*. What kind of person are you?

There are four basic questions he can ask. They are set out below. Bear in mind that he already has part-answers to these questions. When his answers are complete, he will know enough about you to tell whether he wants you or not.

It is a good plan to look yourself over as if you were your own interviewer. Be as searching as you can about the evidence you produce in support of what you say about yourself. But before you size yourself up, here are the basic questions, with brief notes on what they imply:

(i) *What abilities and aptitudes do you possess?*

Some of your potential will be realized, in the form of intellectual achievements and practical skills; some will not yet be fully developed. Combinations of 'hand and brain'. Interests and aptitudes go strikingly together, so questions about interests may give useful clues about your aptitudes.

(ii) *How well do you get on with others?*

Immediate impression; appearance, grooming, speech, manner: 'impact'; the experience of people who have formed your acquaintance, of your friends, of those who depend on you, look up to you, take orders from you, etc. Your own view of your relationships.

(iii) *What motivates you?*

Aims you set yourself; steps taken to achieve these aims; how you cope with obstacles.

(iv) *How do you react to your environment?*

Fitting in among people, and in an organization; stability in situations of change, tension, etc.

Size Yourself Up

This isn't a game, nor even a quiz. There can't be a score, because although some qualities (character-traits, attitudes, etc.) are necessary in every human setting, others only become important according to the needs of a particular job. Often, it is a combination of qualities that matters, not those qualities in isolation. You don't look for leadership, for example, in those on the bottom rung of the ladder (though followership has its qualities too). You wouldn't be very impressed by a middle-rung aspirant who can give orders and see that they are carried out, but doesn't readily take orders himself.

To some of the questions below there are no 'right' answers. When you try to answer them you will see why. (The first half-dozen questions are cases in point. There are others dotted about, too.) The answer that the interviewer is after will come, in these cases, either from his interpretation of what you 'really' mean, or from your answer to a follow-up question.

1. *Are you happy in your work?*

   You may be happy because you are in a rut, or because you find work challenging and stimulating.

   You may be unhappy because the work is tiresome and undemanding, or it is more than you can reasonably cope with.

2. *Are you always on the go?*

   You may be a hard worker, but you could be working yourself to death and causing tension in those around you; your own hard work may lead you to expect too much of others.

   You may find it hard to relax because you think that relaxing proves that you are losing your grip.

3. *Can you bear anyone to disagree with you?*

You may be on the defensive, a bit unsure of yourself.

You may be over-confident, and find it hard to accept that you might possibly be wrong.

4. *Do you take too much on?*

You may be a willing horse, or you may lack the courage to say 'No'.

You may enjoy tackling a tough assignment, or you may not realize your limitations.

5. *Does success go to your head?*

You may be capable of doing better, but decide to rest on your reputation.

You may be unable to accept failure, and so set yourself unrealistic targets.

6. *Do you 'pass the buck'?*

You may say 'It isn't my job' to relieve yourself of responsibility.

Or you may hang on to jobs because you can't bear to see others bungle them.

Aggression

Do you ever lose your temper?

When did you last feel 'I've heard enough of their arguments. I must put them right'?

Do you ever lay down the law to your friends?

What do you do if you can't get your way?

What would you be prepared to do to achieve some aim that is important to you?

Getting on with people

Are you a good mixer?

In the give-and-take of everyday life, do you think you matter as much as most people you mix with?

Do people notice you?

Do they respect your opinions?

Do you think that people trust you?

If you had a good idea, and put it forward to a group of your friends, how would it go down?

If an important decision was to be made by a body you belong to, would other members ask your opinion?

Are you a good 'committee man'?

Can you catch other people's eyes easily?

Would they bother to catch yours?

Do people agree with your point of view more often than not?

Do you have opinions, but keep quiet about them?

Have you many friends?

Are you a nervous person?

Do you 'go with the crowd'?

Do you ever 'go it alone'?

Can you enthuse other people?

Do you enjoy meeting the public (or new people)?

Do you possess leadership qualities?

Do you find it difficult to make your mind up?

Do you often change your mind?

Can you give orders (or express a point of view, or make an explanation) briefly and clearly?

Do people understand what you say to them?

Do they argue the point?

Can you get people to work quickly and willingly for you?

Are you able to demonstrate what you want others to do?

Could you yourself do what you demand of others?

Do you have to assert yourself to make your presence felt?

Are you an official of any body you belong to?

Can you give an example or two of leadership you have exercised in a setting similar to that in the job for which you are applying?

A mixed bag of questions

(do you think any of them unfair?)

Are you an extrovert or an introvert (or a bit of both)?

Would you call yourself observant?

What have you done lately that you are proud of?

Are there any faults that you think you possess?

Can you take responsibility?

Are you good at handling money?

Can you admit to making a mistake? And retrieve the situation gracefully and effectively?

Have you ever cheated?

Do you possess initiative?

Can you work without supervision?

Do you need a lot of encouragement?

Do you give up easily?

Do you need watching?

Are you apt to waste time?

Are you well-balanced?

Can you grasp ideas (methods, what a situation needs) quickly?

Have you the personal resource to cope with ... (a problem related to your job)?

Are you rather an emotional person?

Are you a difficult person to work with?

Do you rub people up the wrong way?

Are you trustworthy?

Are you a person of principle? What happens when your principles are hard to achieve?

Can you achieve effective working compromises with people in order to get things done?

How do you react in situations of strain?

Are you a 'character'?

Can you learn from experience?

Are you a good organizer?

Are you a good judge of people?

Could you offer evidence to back up your answers?

(Did you think any of the questions unfair?
 If so, there's nothing you can do about it!)

Do You Belong to a Special Category?

Most applicants for a post, or a place in College or University, offer pretty well what is expected of them. In any large bunch of applicants, however, there are bound to be a few who do not fall into the normal category. This can happen for quite innocent reasons, and is not always to the disadvantage of the applicant.

Special applicants usually need special consideration, and questions to such applicants (and inquiries made about them too) are likely to be exceptionally probing.

Among candidates in a special category are the following. Are you, for example:

One who is rather older (or rather younger) than most recruits to the job.

> The interviewer may wonder whether you are older and therefore insufficiently adaptable, or younger and insufficiently experienced.

One with fewer than the asked-for qualifications.

> Why apply, then? Is some quality or experience offered which is a good substitute for the missing qualification? Is this just a try-on, in the hope that the field is so small that personality rather than qualifications will get the job?

One who has stayed too long in one job (or has drifted from job to job).

> The right sort of person? Too set in someone else's ways? Will re-training be a problem? Is the candidate's heart really in this application?

One who was dismissed from his previous place (or has had applications elsewhere rejected, or is rather hopelessly putting applications in here, there, and everywhere.)

> Can we afford other people's rejects? Is he worth interviewing at all?

One with theoretical knowledge but no practical experience (or vice versa).

Has he had the chance to make up the deficiency but passed the opportunity by? Does he expect us to fill the gap for him?

A woman applying for a job usually done by a man (or vice versa).

This is less of a hindrance than it used to be. Employers are becoming much more open-minded and anyway we are not supposed to discriminate. It could be an interesting and worthwhile possibility.

One who has come from abroad with qualifications (or experience, or both) which are not quite relevant here.

Is he worth the risk? Would he fit in?

One who is 'changing course' and making almost a new career for himself.

Why?

One with an unfortunate record: a handicap, long unemployment (or marking time in some inappropriate occupation), ill-health, an ex-prisoner, etc.

Despite the record, is he a worth-while risk? Can we help him? Can he help us?

A woman who is seeking work (or to continue her earlier kind of work) after bringing up a family.

Is she a poor prospect set against better qualified youngsters? Or is her greater maturity and experience a positive asset?

Another example, which is normal and certainly not a special category except in an extreme case, is worth including here because it too, may need special probing questions:

One who has come from a different firm (or public authority, etc.) with different ways of doing things.

Is he adaptable? Is his experience going to be an asset, or will he feel – and let us know he feels – that his former way of doing things is right, and ours are wrong?

Can You Get By on Charm?

A lot of people think you can. They believe that honest merit is often overlooked in favour of pleasing and rather superficial manners. These manners, they think, are a gift of nature to some lucky people, who have discovered that they can succeed with them while others, more hardworking and talented than the charmers, are overlooked.

What is charm? Dictionaries aren't much help. It is a quality that is almost indefinable, but we can easily recognize those who are fortunate enough to possess it. It includes ease of manner, assurance, smoothness in dealing with people – and these are all 'pluses'.

It wouldn't do to assume that those who possess these polished, engaging qualities have little else to offer. If the interviewer can't separate the superficial from what has some depth to it, then he is not up to his job.

Some people are extroverts and some are introverts. The former are the sociable ones. This category includes the show-offs, the life-and-soul-of-the-party types, and all those who shine in company. Public figures are nearly all extroverts.

Introverts include those who prefer their own company, 'shrinking violets', 'social isolates', 'bookish' people, and those who do not need much company to pursue their interests and get on.

The out-and-out extrovert would be an embarrassingly tiresome person, claiming everyone's attention and feeling wretched if he were not at the centre of affairs.

The out-and-out introvert, going his own way and positively shunning company, would be eccentric and almost impossible to get on with.

We are all a bit of a mixture, but most of us incline more to the one than the other. The charmer, by his nature, inclines to extroversion, and if an interviewer accepted his charms too readily he would be overlooking the quieter qualities of those less ready to display themselves.

There can be no doubt, though, that the interview situation is more ready-made for the extrovert than the introvert. The introvert would be asking for trouble if he left it entirely to his interviewer to discover his qualities. An interview is a partnership, and even the introvert must put what he offers on show.

Prejudice in the Interview

Are interviews ever decided on 'hunches'? Does an interviewer turn one candidate down, thinking 'There's something about him I don't like', or accept another with the thought 'I took to him at once'?

Of course an interview can be decided on a hunch. It would be unrealistic to deny this. Every interviewer, like all other human beings, has his prejudices, and he cannot leave them outside the room where he sits in his formal capacity. But at least he can be aware that he is as liable to be prejudiced as the next man, and try to allow for this.

He can standardize his questions and his methods sufficiently to gather comparable information from all those he interviews, so that he doesn't, through prejudice, omit some questions which might have thrown a different, and better, light on an interviewee who doesn't create an immediately favourable impression. He must be flexible too, and ask follow-up questions which develop out of answers to earlier ones.

One common-sense safeguard against prejudice on the part of an individual interviewer is to have a second interviewer, or a panel of interviewers. It is possible, of course, for a whole panel to be prejudiced: they may get on well together and value each other's judgement simply because they have a common background of experience, of education, and of prejudice.

If we tried to devise a method of interviewing which came near to ironing out prejudice, we should almost certainly find that it was so standardized, objective, soulless, and inhumane that its operation would produce worse results than the system it sought to cure.

One form of prejudice is the 'Old Boy network' or the influence of the 'Old School tie'. This is probably much rarer than is generally supposed but can be used as an excuse by disgruntled candidates who can claim (in their own minds) that their failure was due to no fault of their own but to 'privileges' enjoyed by another. But where it is thought to operate, there is nothing the candidate can do about it – except to the extent that it may put him on his mettle.

If he goes into the interview already disgruntled, he is likely to come out dissatisfied. If he goes in in a more positive frame of mind, it is at least on the cards that his interviewer will think twice about rejecting him.

More insidious than this form of prejudice is the so-called 'halo effect'. This happens when interviewer and candidate hit it off because they discover that they have important interests (values, experiences, etc.) in common.

The candidate, having acquired a halo for certain things to his credit, is looked at especially favourably for other things too.

An interviewer has to repress himself to some extent. It would be quite improper for him to steal the limelight. He may need to repress himself still more if he finds himself warming to a candidate simply because of shared interests that may have precious little to do with the job.

Promises, Promises

An interview is nothing if not an exercise in communication.

Yet situations sometimes arise when a candidate (and sometimes an interviewer) thinks back to the interview and wonders what exactly *was* said.

An interviewer would be inexperienced or careless if he did not take proper on-the-spot notes, however brief, of this highly important transaction. Notes are kept 'for the record'; they are available if queries arise, or to pass on to colleagues who have an interest in appointments. They provide useful information when decisions are made about minimum qualifications and other basic matters. Records, as a whole, show how the type of candidate coming forward changes in the course of years. Interview notes are extremely helpful if the selected candidate decides, after all, not to take up the appointment. There is no need to hold another round of interviews: his notes jog the interviewer's memory when he looks for the 'second string'.

The candidate has no such notes to refresh his memory. If he wonders later what promotion prospects were held out to him, how is he to dredge the facts up from a confused memory of so much said in such a short space of time?

Alternatively, he may have come away with a very clear idea of promises made to him, but when they are not fulfilled he has no way of checking whether the words he thought he heard bear the construction he is so anxious to place upon them. Disappointments and allegations of bad faith can easily stem from the lack of a written record. Difficulties can arise about pay, conditions, prospects, duties, the use of a car, the work-location, or a number of other things.

Knowing that difficulties can arise should alert a candidate to take extra care during the interview itself. When critical areas of work and conditions are under discussion, the candidate can help himself by repeating his interviewer's words. 'Now, have I got this right . . .?' By repeating it to the interviewer for confirmation the candidate is more likely to remember it accurately later. Moreover, he lays himself open to immediate correction if he does happen to have got it wrong.

The most difficult areas arise on the question of prospects. An employer may be recruiting a person who, if all goes well, could in a few years' time step into the shoes of a retiring Director or Partner.

But there are bound to be provisos. Obviously the applicant must work well and show the right aptitudes during the intervening period. Or the promotion itself could be less than definite since it might only be given if won against competition from others in the same firm. Or it could be subject to the approval of some large shareholder who might have other ideas and a lot of influence.

It is in circumstances of this kind that the applicant should be absolutely clear as to what he and the interviewer have agreed, and should ask for it to be confirmed in writing, perhaps in a formal letter of appointment. This is particularly important if the promises refer, rather vaguely, to some time in the future, or when they hinge on decisions or policies yet to be finalized. It is precisely in these circumstances, of course, that the interviewer needs to guard himself, so that he cannot be as definite as he would like to be. Many promises must therefore remain at the verbal level.

If promises are made verbally, and are not likely to be referred to in a letter of appointment, it would be well for the candidate to jot them down for his own record, while they are still fresh in his memory, ready to be produced or referred to if ever this becomes necessary.

A candidate may make his share of promises too. He may express his willingness to move house, if necessary, or to follow some course to improve his qualifications, or to be available for duties outside normal hours, etc. He must not be surprised if his employer is as anxious to keep him up to the mark as the other way about.

Definite promises made on both sides should be included in the Contract of Employment, a formal document which by Law must be given to the Employee within 13 weeks of commencement. It lays down the terms and conditions of employment.

Why do Some Candidates Succeed ... and Others Fail?

It is a happy situation when an interviewer realises that, when introductions are over and the candidate is sitting comfortably, there is no need for a warm-up conversation, but the interview can go forward to business straight away. It is a compliment to the candidate too, that he has made an immediate impact. His presence, bearing, maturity, responsiveness, and forthcoming manner have all declared themselves, and he gains as well from the relaxed yet workmanlike atmosphere.

Does it surprise you that an interview can be a pleasure? It shouldn't. When an interview drags, it is because a candidate (or the interviewer!) is reserved, uncertain, ultra-cautious, or plain dull, and the process of breaking down the barriers can be time-consuming and sometimes rather wearing.

It is a welcome surprise when a candidate shows at once that no such process is necessary. In this case, the candidate gains as much as the interviewer does, and the pleasure is reciprocal.

Usually, an interview confirms the impression gained from the written application, but sometimes the face-to-face encounter produces a different impression. This may be because the active personal presence is more positive than a painstakingly written document. Or perhaps, on the other hand, because a candidate finds it easier to be forthcoming on paper than his shyness or inadequacy allows him to be in person.

Undeniably, there is an element of luck in being successful in landing a job (less so, perhaps, in keeping it). A successful application depends on a coincidence: a candidate's knowledge, skill, and personality match reasonably well the job that is going at the time the candidate is free to offer himself.

There is sometimes an element of hard luck when a candidate fails. (But not so often as candidates would have you believe.)

Questions of luck apart, there are some reasons for failure that are well worth considering. The following are some of them:

1. *Qualifications do not match requirements.*

If the difference between qualifications and requirements is too great, the applicant won't be called for interview at all. He has merely aimed at the wrong target.

If the difference is slender, the applicant may be called for interview for one of several reasons: there may be a poor field; or the candidate may be worth seeing because he might possess other qualities or experience to counterbalance the discrepancy; or the discrepancy might be fairly easily remedied by training; or there might be special circumstances of a 'hard luck' nature which make it worthwhile to see him.

2. *Personal qualities do not match requirements.*

The applicant may be immature, or so apparently young for his age that his colleagues, contacts, customers, etc., might not take him sufficiently seriously. He might be dull, unobservant, unresponsive, lacking in ambition and drive. Perhaps experience at school (and later) did not stimulate him sufficiently: perhaps the stimulus was there but he did not accept the challenge.

3. *The candidate creates conditions of failure for himself by not studying the market.*

If he is a candidate for a place at College or University, he may not have informed himself about the subjects prerequisite for the courses he wants to take. If he is an applicant for a job in commerce or industry, and has misjudged the market, he may have over-valued what he has to offer. Is he an incurable optimist? Has panic led him to apply on too wide a front?

Or it may become clear that the applicant has not made any study at all of the Company he is applying to, and knows nothing of its products, its advertisements, or its subsidiaries and their activities. Candidates for top-level appointments need to demonstrate a shrewd assessment of profits/losses and balance sheets, and need to have followed the recent progress and development of the Company sufficiently well to say what it is that they like about it.

4. *The candidate's experience may be inadequate, or of the wrong sort.*

Too many changes of job? Is he a drifter? Why does he think he can make a success of a job with us? Is he flying a kite? Can we wholly trust his description of his previous job successes, or of his reason for leaving earlier jobs? Is he more of a talker than a doer? He is evidently willing to take the risk of switching jobs or taking on something new, but can we afford to take the risk with him?

After some interviews, the interviewer is expected to note down the reasons for failure (perhaps for colleagues, or to pass on to another body interviewing the candidate). What kind of reasons are given?

An out-and-out failure (such as 'He will never make a . . .') is rarely recorded. Nearly always there is something to be said on the positive side. A candidate may be personable, yet unaware of what he would be taking on if he were accepted. He may have developed extremely well a narrow range of talents, and yet show little or no promise in other fields just as vital. He may think his strengths will get him through, and be unaware of the extent of his weaknesses.

'Failures' at interview can never be eliminated, but the number of 'failures' can be reduced by candidates who are prepared to look after their own interests more than some of them do at present. They need to be more realistic and less happy-go-lucky in their applications; they need to study the market more; they need to appraise their own skills and knowledge more carefully (and, often, bring them up-to-date); they need to plan ahead so that gaining qualifications and experience is part of the job-hunting process.

There is so much in job-hunting (and in place-hunting in Colleges and Universities) that a candidate can do for himself that it is surely fruitless to spend time and energy blaming bad luck or the machinations of those who get there before we do for our lack of success. Those who make appointments are bound to be a bit suspicious of candidates with too many excuses, or who are apt to blame anyone but themselves.

Help for the Unemployed

In Great Britain the Government is trying to help the unemployed with various measures which are operated by the Manpower Services Commission. This is a Government agency which is accountable to the Department of Employment. A brief account of the principal schemes is given below and further details are available at Jobcentres.

General Placing Service: This is organized through the Jobcentres which exist in most main towns. Vacancies are displayed on cards, and it is a 'self-service' operation. However, staff are available to give more assistance.

Professional and Executive Recruitment (PER): This caters for managerial, professional, scientific, technical and executive vacancies. It is run as a commercial operation in the sense that it charges fees to employers who use it (and in this respect is similar to non-Government employment agencies). A weekly newspaper is published which carries details of vacancies, and it also provides other information and services for job seekers.

Special Services for Disabled People: This includes schemes and grants for adaptation to premises or equipment, loans of special tools and equipment, assistance for travel expenses and grants for employers who employ disabled people for a trial period.

Employment Rehabilitation: This is for those who have been ill or who are handicapped in some way. These schemes provide, or give financial assistance for, courses which prepare you for work. There are also special schemes to help the educationally sub-normal.

Sheltered Employment: Can be provided for the severely disabled who could not get work otherwise.

The Job Search Scheme: This gives financial assistance to help the unemployed to travel away from home for interviews.

The Employment Transfer Scheme: This enables some unemployed to get a grant to move home permanently to take up work in a new area – but only where vacancies in that area cannot be filled locally.

The Enterprise Allowance Scheme: This only works in pilot areas where there may be an allowance to help unemployed people who want to start up in business.

The Community Programme: This provides temporary local full – or part-time jobs for longer term unemployed adults doing work which benefits the community. The range of work includes environmental improvement, provision of social amenities or other social or cultural work. The appropriate local 'rate for the job' is paid to workers, and a MSC subsidy is provided to the employer. All recruitment for this scheme is through Jobcentres, Careers Offices or PER.

Training Opportunities Scheme (TOPS): This provides courses for training, retraining or preparation for work. These are held in colleges, MSC Skillcentres or sometimes in employers' establishments.

Youth Training Scheme (see page 61): Is organized through career officers.

Things to do ...

Dress the part; act the part.

You owe it to yourself to show that you appreciate what will be expected of you if your application is accepted. Is this 'putting on an act'? Not really. If you can't look as you should do in the interview, is it likely that you will do so when working? You don't want to leave your interviewer wondering whether you are casual and don't care, or whether you are simply unaware of what your application implies.

Be yourself.

Obviously. But you are more than one 'self', aren't you? Or, at least, there are different sides to yourself, and you might as well show the most favourable one. An interview is a matching process. You have to show that you fit the vacancy, the place at College, or wherever the interview leads. You have to do this without giving a false, or strained, impression, and this can only happen if the interviewer sees the real 'you'. If he suspects a façade, he will try to dismantle it. You have been warned!

Show some enthusiasm.

This is clearly a necessity, yet some candidates – perhaps because they are overawed by a sense of occasion – sit stodgily there and don't do any sort of justice to themselves. After all, you *did* apply, and this argues some keenness. Now keep it up.

Things to avoid ...

Don't appear sour or disgruntled, or behave as if you bear a grudge or have an axe to grind.

Try to be confident and at least mildly optimistic. Some candidates give an unfortunate impression with lengthy explanations of why they were right and someone else wrong – perhaps in a former job. This looks too much like defensive self-justification. Keep yourself in check if you think you are liable to blame other people, argue with your interviewer, or press a point of view too strongly.

Don't appear over-confident, or boastful.

Exaggerated claims invite doubt, and perhaps incredulity. They lead to searching follow-up questions, and an uncomfortable feeling of deflation for you. One of the worst things you can do is to give the impression that you know your interviewer's business better than he does.

If ...

If you were rejected ...

What did you learn from the encounter?

Were you surprised by the decision?

Was there an element of bad luck?

Was there a stage when you felt things begin to go wrong?

Did you hit it off with the interviewer?

Did you sense any sort of barrier between you and the interviewer?

Is there anything you could do about poor communication?

Did any questions take you by surprise?

It's no use blaming the interviewer for failure. He may have been inexperienced, biased, careless (and whatever other derogatory adjectives you care to add) but with all his limitations, he is a fact for you to reckon with. (If he is as bad as you might think, his employers and associates will suffer

If you were accepted ...

Don't let your new-won confidence on acceptance go to your head. You still have to make a start at the job itself.

If you made any promises at interview, or expressed hopes for the future, don't be surprised to be taken at your word.

Success on this occasion should encourage you to try further in due course.

If you were rejected ...   **If you were accepted ...**

from his poor decisions.) At least you have experienced a useful and crucial exercise in human relations. Don't let one unfortunate experience deter you from offering your services elsewhere. At the same time, don't forget that your recent interviewer has his view of the situation. Perhaps he is not as bad – or you as good – as you think. If you are prepared to be self-critical you might offer a more streamlined version of yourself to the next interviewer.

Honestly, were you adequately prepared? If not, you can help yourself to better 'luck' next time.

Whatever you do, don't lose heart.

Index

OUR PUBLISHING POLICY

HOW WE CHOOSE

Our policy is to consider every deserving manuscript and we can give special editorial help where an author is an authority on his subject but an inexperienced writer. We are rigorously selective in the choice of books we publish. We set the highest standards of editorial quality and accuracy. This means that a *Paperfront* is easy to understand and delightful to read. Where illustrations are necessary to convey points of detail, these are drawn up by a subject specialist artist from our panel.

HOW WE KEEP PRICES LOW

We aim for the big seller. This enables us to order enormous print runs and achieve the lowest price for you. Unfortunately, this means that you will not find in the *Paperfront* list any titles on obscure subjects of minority interest only. These could not be printed in large enough quantities to be sold for the low price at which we offer this series.

We sell almost all our *Paperfronts* at the same unit price. This saves a lot of fiddling about in our clerical departments and helps us to give you world-beating value. Under this system, the longer titles are offered at a price which we believe to be unmatched by any publisher in the world.

OUR DISTRIBUTION SYSTEM

Because of the competitive price, and the rapid turnover, *Paperfronts* are possibly the most profitable line a bookseller can handle. They are stocked by the best bookshops all over the world. It may be that your bookseller has run out of stock of a particular title. If so, he can order more from us at any time—we have a fine reputation for "same day" despatch, and we supply any order, however small (even a single copy), to any bookseller who has an account with us. We prefer you to buy from your bookseller, as this reminds him of the strong underlying public demand for *Paperfronts*. Members of the public who live in remote places, or who are housebound, or whose local bookseller is unco-operative, can order direct from us by post.

FREE

If you would like an up-to-date list of all paperfront titles currently available, send a stamped self-addressed envelope to
ELLIOT RIGHT WAY BOOKS, BRIGHTON RD.,
LOWER KINGSWOOD, SURREY, U.K.